Safeguarding Intangible Assets

T0348532

Safeguarding
Intangible Assets

Michael D. Moberly

AMSTERDAM • BOSTON • HEIDELBERG • LONDON
NEW YORK • OXFORD • PARIS • SAN DIEGO
SAN FRANCISCO • SINGAPORE • SYDNEY • TOKYO
Butterworth-Heinemann is an imprint of Elsevier

Acquiring Editor: *Brian Romer*
Editorial Project Manager: *Keira Bunn*
Project Manager: *Punithavathy Govindaradjane*
Designer: *Russell Purdy*

Butterworth-Heinemann is an imprint of Elsevier
The Boulevard, Langford Lane, Kidlington, Oxford, OX5 1GB, UK
225 Wyman Street, Waltham, MA 02451, USA

Copyright © 2014 Elsevier Inc. All rights reserved.

No part of this publication may be reproduced, stored in a retrieval system or transmitted
in any form or by any means electronic, mechanical, photocopying, recording or otherwise
without the prior written permission of the publisher.

Permissions may be sought directly from Elsevier's Science & Technology Rights
Department in Oxford, UK: phone (+44) (0) 1865 843830; fax (+44) (0) 1865 853333;
email: permissions@elsevier.com. Alternatively you can submit your request online by
visiting the Elsevier web site at http://elsevier.com/locate/permissions, and selecting
Obtaining permission to use Elsevier material

Notice
No responsibility is assumed by the publisher for any injury and/or damage to persons
or property as a matter of products liability, negligence or otherwise, or from any use or
operation of any methods, products, instructions or ideas contained in the material herein.
Because of rapid advances in the medical sciences, in particular, independent verification
of diagnoses and drug dosages should be made.

Library of Congress Cataloging-in-Publication Data

Moberly, Michael D.
  Safeguarding intangible assets / Michael D. Moberly.
    pages cm
  ISBN 978-0-12-800516-3
1. Corporate culture. 2. Organizational behavior. 3. Intangible property. 4. Reputation.
5. Value. I. Title.
  HD58.7.M6253 2014
  659.2–dc23

                                                                              2014009832

British Library Cataloguing-in-Publication Data
A catalogue record for this book is available from the British Library

For information on all Butterworth-Heinemann
publications visit our website at http://store.elsevier.com

This book has been manufactured using Print On Demand technology. Each copy is
produced to order and is limited to black ink. The online version of this book will show
color figures where appropriate.

Working together
to grow libraries in
developing countries

www.elsevier.com • www.bookaid.org

Contents

About the Author

Michael D. Moberly is an intangible asset strategist and risk specialist and president and founder of Knowledge Protection Strategies, intersecting intangible assets and business. Mike has more than 25 years of experience in matters specifically related to intangible assets, i.e.,

Mike served as a professor at Southern Illinois University at Carbondale (1982– 2002) and adjunct professor in Webster University's MBA program. Mike brings strong national and international experiences, operational insights, a strong research regimen, and respectful communication skills to his engagements.

Business differentiators lie in Mike's (a.) recognition how intangibles originate, develop, mature, and become embedded in company practices and processes and are *in play* in most every business transaction, new project, or operation, and (b.) distinctive approach to asset assessment, development, due diligence, training, research, publishing, training, teaching, and consulting.

Because intangibles have become globally universal 'building blocks' for most company's value, sources of revenue, and sustainability, Mike's work focuses on the fiduciary and fiscal imperative to guide company management teams to achieve effective asset stewardship, oversight, and management, i.e.,

- Identify, unravel, develop, and engage their intangible assets.
- Monitor asset value, materiality, and risk.
- Sustain control, use, and ownership of intangibles.
- Conduct asset assessments and due diligence in both pre and post transaction contexts.

Mike has published numerous articles related to intangibles for Intellectual Asset Management and Security Management respectively, and co-authored a comprehensive paper on university technology transfer. Readers are encouraged to search Mike's 'Business IP and Intangible Asset Blog', now routinely read in 137countries, for posts which supplement issues addressed in this book, i.e., http://kpstrat.com/blog.

Mike has conducted more than 75 national and international presentations, including on air subject matter expert pieces for NPR, CNBC, and CNN, as well as training seminars for professional associations, early stage firms, startups, small-medium size enterprises, and corporate-university (research) alliances. In addition, Mike serves as program and outreach chair for the Intangible Asset Finance Society and is a longtime member of ASIS International's Information Asset Protection Council for which he was recognized as Council Chairperson of the year for 2013.

Mike holds BA and MPA degrees from Indiana University along with hours toward a doctoral degree in political science. He previously held positions in the Federal Bureau of Prisons and Indiana Department of Corrections.

Acknowledgments

I wish to dedicate this book to Deb, who has consistently been an unwavering source of encouragement and support allowing me to pursue this and other aspirations. Deb is also the epitome of a blind date that took place 42 years ago that culminated in my good fortune of finding a spouse well above my station.

I also would like to thank Pop, who always believed in me and my work and tried his best to familiarize his coffee-drinking and mall-walking friends with intangible assets and intellectual property. And, equally important to Faye, my mother, who would have merely said, 'I always knew you would get it done eventually, I had faith'!

Also, I extend my genuine appreciation to Laurie Washington and Allison Krepel who I could count on to provide respectful assistance, initially as law school students, and now as successful attorneys in their own right.

And lastly, I wish to extend a special appreciation to Elsevier editors' Keira Bunn and Punithavathy Govindaradja, whose consistently respectful, patient, and professional demeanor along with their experienced guidance and suggestions, were always on target to make this book better.

Introduction

In no other arena of economic and social relations has the statement "knowledge is power" proven more true than in today's knowledge-based global economies wherein business operations are increasingly dominated by the creation, utilization, and conversion of intangible assets. Monitoring value, materiality, and risk to intangible assets throughout their functionality life cycle is now a managerial requisite!

How It All Began

I can genuinely say that my 25 years' of research, work, and consulting on a broad cross-section of matters related to identifying, safeguarding, and managing intangible assets evolved more as an epiphany. The epiphany occurred in the late 1990s while I was on the faculty at Southern Illinois University at Carbondale (1982–2002) where I taught and conducted research in an academic unit, which at the time was named the Center for the Study of Crime, Delinquency, and Corrections. In the late 1980s I had the good fortune of being encouraged by my department chair to develop and introduce into the curriculum a course that focused exclusively on the rapidly expanding private security industry, a task and responsibility that I eagerly accepted.

Those familiar with the private security industry during this early developmental and rapid-growth period in the 1980s and 1990s understand that the industry was frequently and disparagingly characterized as constituting "guards, guns, and gates." Its employees were characterized as "rent-a-cops" or "police officer wannabes." At the time, there were few insights, knowledge, or research about the proprietary side of private security, which is most commonly associated with corporate security. Television and movies only added to the role confusion between private security and public law enforcement. There was no shortage of programs in which a private investigator was the central character who seemed to consistently skirt the law and engage in gratuitous violence and quasi–law enforcement activities absent, in most instances, of any legal repercussions.

With these challenges in mind, I set about designing this new course. One of my objectives was to identify emerging global risks and threats to companies that in turn would place a premium on more specialized security services—in other words, demonstrate viable paths for transitioning from being a security generalist to a security specialist. The popularity and favorable assessments of my initial security course warranted the development and delivery of two additional and higher-level security courses. It was these two courses that would be dominated by the subject of intangible assets—that is, know-how and intellectual, structural, and relationship capital.

Emergence and Integration of Intangible Assets

Intangible (nonphysical) assets had, after all, quite literally replaced conventional business economies that had for hundreds of years evolved around the production and utilization of tangible (physical) assets. This economic transformation began in the mid to late 1990s and started to influence business decision makers, management teams, and boards globally to rethink their business strategies to include identifying and profitably exploiting their intangible assets that formed the origins of most companies' value, sources of revenue, and competitive advantages.

What was exactly new about this knowledge-based global economy was debatable, says Dr. Baruch Lev, a business economist at New York University. But, one feature of the 21st century became crystal clear: intangible assets were playing an increasingly important and integral role in most company's value, competitive advantages, and wealth-creation potential.

Dr. Lev also states that economic activity increasingly consists of the exchange of ideas, information, expertise, and know-how, which are, of course, intangible assets. Thus, company value, profitability, and sustainability are being driven by a company's collective competencies and capabilities to exploit its intangible assets than by control over or use of physical resources or tangible assets.

Even the value of tangible goods is often based on integrating intangible assets, such as technical innovations, which are routinely embedded in a company's products or services through intellectual and structural capital, including brand, creative presentation, and content (adapted from the work of Dr. Baruch Lev (2005), NYU.)

Thus, in today's increasingly intangible asset–dominated global business environment, it's inevitable that intangible assets will play an increasingly significant role in most transactions. This means achieving consistent business success is now inextricably linked to the effective stewardship, oversight, and management of intangible assets, including the ability to:

- Identify and assess intangible assets' collective and individual contributory values.
- Sustain control, use, and ownership of the assets throughout their life, value, and functionality cycles.
- Produce, develop, position, leverage, and extract value from intangible assets.

- Understand how to exploit intangible assets' contributory and collaborative elements and the competitive advantages they produce.
- Monitor intangible assets' value, materiality, and risk in both pre– and post–business transaction contexts, and in designing and executing exit strategies.

My Purpose for Writing This Book

The purpose of this book is embedded in the reality that increasing percentages of company value and revenue lay in intangible assets, regardless of a company's size, location, maturation, or industry sector. Management and oversight of a company's intangible assets are no longer solely legal or accounting processes; rather they are business decisions. The stewardship, oversight, and management of a company's intangible assets have permanently shifted from being optional tasks—something that gets done as time permits, as resources become available, or when competitors are observed doing it—to fiduciary responsibilities that can no longer be dismissed, neglected, or relegated to the uninitiated.

This book also dispels the myth that intangible assets and their management is the sole province of large, multinational corporations. More accurately, intangible assets are firmly embedded in and being routinely produced by the 20+ million small, midsize, and early-stage firms in the United States and an equal number globally, regardless of industry sector.

To maximize reader benefits, each chapter is designed to be a quick read that delivers numerous multipliers for time-constrained readers. For example, each chapter brings operational clarity to particular aspects of intangible asset management by:

- Treating the management of intangible assets as business decisions and fiduciary responsibilities, not solely as legal or accounting processes.
- Structuring business transactions to mitigate risks that can entangle intangible assets in costly and time-consuming legal disputes, disrupt project momentum, and undermine projected synergies and competitive advantages.
- Building and fostering a company culture that supports the collaborative value of intangible assets.
- Aligning (reframing) contingency planning to be more organizationally resilient and include intangible assets.
- Ensuring the production and contributory role and value of intangible assets is aligned with a company's core mission, strategic planning, and the types of transactions typically engaged.
- Elevating company reputation, image, and goodwill among a broad range of stakeholders, and gain attention of audiences beyond a company's traditional market space.

- Reducing asset vulnerability to acts of theft and misappropriation (risks, threats), which when materialized, will undermine asset value, competitive advantages, market position, and adversely affect reputation.
- Exploitation of intangible assets commensurate with their life, value, and functionality cycles.

So, whether you elect to read this book in its entirety or select particular chapters that reflect a current problem and bring practical insights for solving that problem, my message remains laser-focused: business decision makers, regardless of their specialization, professional experiences, or title, need to acquire operational and managerial familiarity with intangible assets because these skill sets are now requisites for successfully and effectively managing intangible asset–dominated companies, regardless of size, location, sector, or maturity.

Homegrown Intangible Assets

I recognize that most every company possesses what I often refer to as "homegrown" (i.e., internally produced and company-specific) intangible assets that are specialized or distinctively relevant to a company irrespective of its location, size, industry sector, or maturity. In many, if not most instances, however, intangible assets may not be particularly well suited to one-size-fits-all managerial or company culture circumstances. Instead, they may require nuanced modification and handling aligned with, achieving the most effective and efficient use, maximizing their collaborative value, building and strengthening a company's structural capital and competitive advantages throughout its supply-value chain, and specific types of business transactions a company most frequently engages.

Therefore, this book advocates practical and individualized approaches to utilizing, bundling, and managing intangible assets, which I refer to as the "what fits best tends to work best" strategy. More specifically, my experience suggests that what fits best for a company and its operating culture will usually work best for that company to achieve its business goals and objectives.

This book also does not require readers to step outside their primary areas of expertise to understand and apply the various principles and strategies presented. Instead, the book is designed to build on readers' existing expertise by adding challenging, relevant, and forward-looking dimensions to their areas of specialization and expertise. I believe this approach that respects achievements of management team members helps companies proceed more quickly with their competitiveness, profitability, and being less vulnerable to the ever-growing array of risks and threats that can rapidly materialize to literally sap the value from intangible assets and undermine and erode their competitive advantages.

I am a strong advocate of utilizing intangible assets as fully and completely as possible. However, I caution readers to not characterize intangible assets as constituting either the proverbial "silver bullet" or a one-size-fits-all template for success. That is why each chapter in this book provides readers with relevant and current insights about not just a starting point, but the practical steps that are necessary to ensure companies arrive at a successful, profitable, and strategically sustainable destination and outcome.

Value and Functionality of Intangible Assets Can Fluctuate

Admittedly, the value and functionality of intangible assets can fluctuate, sometimes quite rapidly. In other words, intangible assets can be perishable and nonrenewable, somewhat akin to purchasing fresh fruit or vegetables from a grocery. The "shelf life" of either, if not kept in optimal conditions, can be brief. The consumable value can succumb to spoilage and be irrevocably lost.

To be sure, there are similarities, and even perhaps some overlap with practices related to identifying, monitoring, and safeguarding intangible assets. Advisedly, there should be some degree of flexibility and maneuverability built into each practice to accommodate the nuances and idiosyncrasies of particular intangible assets and to reflect the assets' value, functionality, obsolescence cycle, and propensity to risk.

That said, conventional checklist types of asset risk assessments (e.g., audits, due diligence, and valuation), when conducted by the uninitiated, often turn out to be merely snapshots in time and do not reveal the strategic, dynamic, and over-the-horizon level of insight that is so essential for reflecting today's ultracompetitive and predatorial business transaction environments.

That's because, in large part, risks and threats to intangible assets are asymmetric and materialize in an array of frequently business-crippling contexts as well as inadvertent or purposeful acts, not the least of which are infringement, theft, misappropriation, and economic (industrial) espionage. Also, intangible assets' risk—that is, their vulnerability to, the probability of, and the criticality of a materialized risk—elevates in proportion to an asset's value, the competitive advantages it produces, and its commercialization or monetization potential.

Intangible Assets: Tested, Practical, and Valuable

I routinely have the opportunity to engage a cross-section of business leaders, management team members, and entrepreneurs about my favorite topics: identifying, unraveling, assessing, commercializing, and safeguarding intangible assets. One of my colleagues recently suggested that the development, use, and exploitation of intangible assets remain largely theoretical. (Unfortunately, there remain some audiences who are inclined to crudely characterize theories as merely constituting an academic's guess, hunch, untested opinion, or supposition.)

Having taught in universities for more than 25 years, and now being an intangible asset strategist and risk specialist, I can say, unequivocally, that a significant percentage of the time when I utter the word "theory" in a classroom or during a presentation at a professional association meeting, the fairly consistent initial reactions I observe, whether it emanates from high-caliber graduate students or astute and experienced business persons, are variations of a muffled sigh, as if to say, we're going to take a nap now while the speaker tries to explain a theory that we're already inclined to presume has little, if any, relevance to the real business world.

My reaction has been to adapt my classroom and business presentations to characterize theories somewhat differently, by pointing out first that theories—be they about intangible assets or other issues—are thoughtful and generally well-researched explanations regarding a particular behavior or phenomena. This definitional prelude resonates much better with audiences.

Still, it remains frustrating to hear otherwise intelligent, experienced, savvy, and successful business persons or grad students express a dismissive attitude toward intangible assets, or worse, reject the globally recognized economic facts regarding intangible assets by characterizing them as unsubstantiated theories that will not hold up to the scrutiny, rigors, and stresses of today's ultra-aggressive, competitive, and "go hard, go fast, go global" business transaction environment.

The inclusion of intangible assets in business valuation and management is, to be sure, a more comprehensive and, I might add, correct approach to accurately describe (qualitatively and quantitatively) a company's real value, its sources of revenue, its growth potential, its profitability, and its overall stability. Thus, to respectfully appeal to the various business persons who remain reluctant or skeptical about actually engaging and applying intangible assets to their business and nuanced circumstances, what follows are real definitions, categories, and examples of intangible assets!

I recognize that just making sense of the knowledge-based (intangible asset) economy and business environment is not sufficient unless readers can use and apply the information provided in this book to frame and execute their own roadmap. That's why the various chapters in the book will individually and collectively provide readers with relevant and current insights about the practical steps that are necessary to help produce a successful, profitable, and strategically sustainable roadmap.

Intangible assets frequently fall under the purview of conventional MBA programs or business schools. This has, in essence, sanctioned tolerance for numerous management teams to express little interest in or seek familiarity with the intangible asset side of their business that is often rooted in one or a variation of the following:

- Expressions of self-deprecation—that is, perceptions that their company neither produces nor possesses any intangible assets of value and thus is yet to engage the knowledge-based economy.
- An absence of time, resources, and expertise within their company to engage in strategies to convert intangible assets to revenue, value, or competitive advantages.
- Intangible assets are seldom, if ever, reported on balance sheets or financial statements.

An important initial step to achieving a more intangible asset–conscious business community is to bring more operational clarity and delineation of the benefits derived by identifying and exploiting these assets.

Recognizing the necessity to engage and exploit their intangible assets or determine their contributory value and performance is unfortunately and frequently perceived as being unnecessary or not justifiable, even though today, increasing percentages of most company's value, sources of revenue, and building blocks for growth, sustainability, and profitability evolve directly from intangible assets. That is an economic fact that absolutely should not be overlooked or disregarded. Even though management teams are unable to necessarily see or touch these assets, intuitively they feel or visualize their presence, absence, or changes, for example, through the erosion of a company's reputation, image, goodwill, intellectual capital, value, market space, and competitive advantages.

Using This Book

For management teams who still remain unconvinced or reluctant to engage their company's intangible assets, I am confident this book will allay those perspectives by helping to identify for intangible assets the value they can potentially deliver, the market share they can help capture, and the competitive advantages they can help create.

Ultimately, developing and using intangible assets effectively are business decisions and fiduciary responsibilities owned by the respective management team. That is why this book is a useful requisite to achieving profitability, success, and sustainability in the knowledge-based global economy.

So, if your company is one of those adversely affected by the recession, there may be no better time to learn more about intangible assets and the various ways they can favorably affect and influence your company when developed, used, and exploited effectively. This, of course, is something I urge readers of this book to consider, before electing to pursue more drastic or less desirable, and quite possibly irreversible, options that many other companies in the United States and globally have already taken. The facts are, intangible assets are permanent, irreversible, and valuable fixtures to most businesses and serve as strong underliers to their success, sustainability, and profitability not only for today but for the foreseeable future.

And, to readers who start reading this book with a sense of dismissiveness or suspicion about intangible assets and the principles and strategies offered to help management teams build, protect, and deliver value from them, I suggest the *value* those assets could potentially deliver, the *market share* those assets could help capture, and the *competitive advantages* those assets could create will not be realized and, in all likelihood, will become diluted, undermined, impaired, or irrevocably lost if left unengaged.

While the knowledge-based economy essentially remains in its early stages, the relevance, importance, and contributory value of intangible assets should not be considered as merely theoretical rhetoric that management teams can afford to dismiss.

I hope you enjoy the book!

Michael D. Moberly

Reference

Lev, B., 2005. Intangible asset concepts and measurements Encyclopedia of Social Measurement, vol. 2. Elsevier.

Chapter 1

Intangible Assets

▮ *Moneyball* and Intangible Assets

The following excerpt reflects a meeting between Oakland Athletics' general manager Billy Beane and the team's scouting director Grady Fuson from the film *Moneyball* regarding the famed "Moneyball" draft of 2002:

> *Fuson*: This isn't how you run a ball club, with a computer. You know that. You're a baseball man. There are *intangibles* [emphasis added] that only a scout can see in a player that you're not going to pick up with just numbers, with someone who doesn't play the game, who knows nothing about the game but how to feed numbers into a computer.

> *Beane*: That's what we're doing. That's exactly what we're doing.

> *Fuson*: If this is what baseball is, if it's not Kirk Gibson going up to the plate on two bad legs because the manager felt in his heart that he had one swing left in that body … a computer wouldn't do that. They would have had him sitting up in the stands.

Beane: A computer doesn't romanticize the sport. Leave that for the fans.

(IMSDb, 2011))

Similar to Fuson's perspectives, intangible asset strategists and risk specialists, like myself, have an attitude about the way many management teams and companies conduct business and engage in transactions without regard for the intangible assets they are producing and will inevitably be in play, and the economic fact that 80% or more of most companies' value, sources of revenue, and building blocks for growth, profitability, and sustainability today lie in or evolve directly from intangible assets (Blair and Wallen, 1998–2000; Blair and Wallman, 2001). It's no longer business as usual!

Intangible Assets: The Unseen, Underused, and Undervalued Elephant in The Room

Unfortunately for many companies, their intangible assets remain *the* overlooked, underused, and undervalued economic and competitive-advantage elephant sitting unnoticed, unattended, and unclearly defined in conference rooms globally.

A puzzling aspect to this is that most business stakeholders and constituents, up and down a respective value chain, have experienced some adverse effect or fallout due to an inability, unwillingness, or haphazard manner to effectively engage, safeguard, and utilize their company's intangible assets.

Intangible assets are blends or combinations of procedures, practices, relationships, and culture. That is, they are the intellectual, structural, and relationship capital embedded in a company's distinctive and oftentimes proprietary operations that create efficiencies, facilitate or enhance internal and external relationships, provide special edges or advantages in a market space, and can be leveraged to differentiate a company from its competitors and thus create value.

HELPING COMPANIES EASE OUT OF THE ECONOMIC DOLDRUMS

I am confident readers will find this book useful in various dimensions, one of which is guiding management teams to ease out of the prolonged economic doldrums many countries are experiencing. However, these recessionary periods are certainly not the sole focal point of the book.

Rather, the book is about profitably engaging the economic and competitive-advantage elephant that's in plain view for every management team, corporate suite, and board to see, capture, and exploit for their company's value, revenue, competitive advantages, and building blocks for future and sustainable growth and profitability.

As respectfully conveyed throughout this book, the intangible asset elephant in the room I repeatedly refer to, if you haven't surmised already, represents the economic fact that more than 80% of most companies' value and revenue lie in or evolve directly from intangible assets, but receive far too little attention.

Like most readers of this book, engaging in research—that is, learning about new and relevant aspects to one's profession and expertise—is part of our daily regimen. In the late 1990s, I read a report from the Brookings Institute titled "The Intangibles Project" with principle investigators Margaret Blair and Steven Wallman. Their work was subsequently compiled into a book titled *Unseen Wealth* published in 2001.

I felt so strongly about this research that was still unfolding that I traveled to Washington, DC, the following week to personally talk with Blair and Wallman. Of the countless and significant takeaways I received from the original report (1999), one stood out among all others. There had been a paradigm shift in businesses globally from tangible assets to intangible assets as the new and overwhelming dominant source of value and revenue.

At the time, I was an assistant professor at Southern Illinois University at Carbondale where I thoroughly enjoyed my teaching and research that focused primarily on issues related to corporate security and asset protection. I recognized, somewhat intuitively, that the findings of Blair and Wallman would, and should, eventually bring changes to the corporate security and asset protection profession in terms of what types of categories of assets corporate security's attention would be drawn to that are more for safeguarding and mitigating risks to a company's intangible assets. Drawing attention and elevating awareness within the corporate security industry to intangible assets has become more than a 20-year passion of mine.

Fast forward to 2014, and, for me, it remains both puzzling and frustrating that this still relatively intangible asset elephant sitting in conference rooms throughout the world, which consistently produces valuable intangible assets, is largely dismissed. Intangible assets are embedded in most companies' practices, procedures, and policies from the shop floor, to the corporate suite, and into the board room in the forms of intellectual, relationship, and structural capital.

Engaging a company's intangible assets is not an unduly challenging task. Rather, it's often a matter of acquiring an operational familiarity with what they are and how to identify them, unravel them, recognize their contributory value, position them, bundle them, and leverage them, all as a prelude to building and extracting sustainable value, revenue, and competitive advantages.

When asked, a significant number of management teams I engage with, will acknowledge varying degrees of familiarity with intangible assets, but they emit signals that suggest, for a host of reasons, they still remain somewhat shaky about developing and executing the necessary strategies to engage and exploit these assets. Or perhaps worse, in my view, they remain unconvinced or dismissive about how their intangible assets can be effectively utilized and exploited to elevate value, develop sources of revenue, and achieve long-term profitability and sustainability.

Intangible Assets Frequently Fall Under Conventional MBA/CPA Radar

In my own assessment, having been in academia full time for more than 25 years, I find this predicament, at least in part, attributable to conventional university business management, marketing, accounting, and the overall MBA curricula, which generally does not include reference to or examination of intangible assets. Or, if the curricula or a particular professor does address intangible assets, they are infrequently characterized as the permanent and irreversible components to the knowledge-led economies that we are in the midst of.

In addition, in accounting curricula particularly, intangible assets are frequently lumped into the proverbial accounting (balance sheet, financial statement) catch-all I refer to as "goodwill" and seldom, if ever, singularly distinguished. In large part that is because, as unfortunate as it may be, internally produced intangible assets are generally not publicly reported.

To paraphrase Dr. Deming's sage advice of the last century, if it can't be measured, it can't be managed. This appears alive and well in companies around the globe with respect to intangible assets. So, it's certainly not a stretch to assume that many management teams sense that if intangible assets' value is not required to be reported on either balance sheets or financial statements, why bother with their management, stewardship, oversight, or valuation?

On the other hand, externally acquired intangible assets are reported differently on balance sheets and financial statements, but generally they're not differentiated in ways that management teams can readily recognize and distinguish their contributory value. Management teams should recognize, however, that company balance sheets and financial statements possess a "rearview mirror" orientation. That is, they are essentially historical documents representing what occurred in the previous quarter or year, whereas intangible assets constitute consistent and forward-looking value points for a company.

That said, I still routinely encounter extraordinarily talented, experienced, and highly successful business persons and entrepreneurs who lack an appreciation for the intangible assets they have developed. In fact, in many instances, otherwise extremely astute business persons and entrepreneurs do not recognize intangible assets exist in forms other than goodwill or, worse, assume intangible assets are synonymous with intellectual properties like patents, trademarks, and copyrights.

To be sure, goodwill and reputation are critical elements to any company's intangible asset portfolio because of the significant value and competitive advantages attached, something that firms like BP, Massey Energy, Toyota, and the financial services sector each independently incurred significant reputation risks due largely to what plaintiffs argue is negligence, that is no adhering to oversight regulations, poor or nonexistent risk management, or purposeful delays in notifying consumers or employees of potentially dangerous situations. That is, their goodwill and reputation can fall dramatically overnight when certain risks that have been overlooked, dismissed, or not effectively addressed materialize in front of people throughout the globe. For example, with the aforementioned companies, their goodwill and reputation took substantial, long-lasting, and, in some instances, irreversible nose dives, primarily because key intangible assets were given short shrift in their risk management and oversight practices.

INTANGIBLE ASSETS ROUTINELY COMPRISE MORE THAN 80% OF MOST COMPANIES' VALUE AND REVENUE

But still, what's amazing, and frustrating, is that even though the economic fact that intangible assets routinely comprise more than 80% of most companies' value and source of revenue today, there remain significant percentages of management teams who are quick to dismiss them and reluctant to engage them. Again, this may have to do with their lack of physicality, or interpreting them as mere addendums to or synonymous with intellectual property as already stated.

A frequently used reason I have heard, however, is the absence of consensus or standardized procedure by a routinely enforced regulatory agency mandate to report or account for the value and performance of intangible assets.

MANAGEMENT TEAMS' SELF-DEPRECATING PERSPECTIVES ABOUT INTANGIBLE ASSETS

Interestingly, on numerous occasions I have heard company management team members express self-deprecating perspectives about any intangible assets their company may produce or possess. This suggests to me, there remain a substantial number of management teams that sense they are not engaged in or far removed from the globally universal intangible asset driven business economy where intangibles can be sources of value, revenue, and competitive advantage.

A partial reason for this is that conventional (company) management education and training influences business persons to assign specific dollar values to assets, intangible or otherwise, albeit largely subjective. However, assessing the (dollar) value of intangibles as standalone assets routinely overlooks the assets' contributory value, i.e., how they collaboratively contribute to other intangibles, e.g., efficiencies, competitive advantages, etc.

Just as frequently overlooked, misunderstood, or misrepresented is the reality that for conventional intellectual property protections (e.g., patents, copyrights, and trademarks), they are no longer consistent indicators of company value, and they can advance a company (economically, competitively, etc.) only so long as the holder can sustain control, use, or ownership, and monitor the value, materiality, and risk to those assets. The holder is solely responsible for their safeguarding against illegal acts such as misappropriation, infringement, and counterfeiting.

PARADIGM SHIFT TO INTANGIBLE ASSETS IS NOT A "BUBBLE" THAT WILL BURST

It's an equally grave error when I hear members of a company's management team trivialize intangible assets and the knowledge-influenced global economy and business transaction environment as being merely constituting new, but temporary marketing jargon, or condescendingly characterize the intangible assets' phenomena in a "bubble" context that will soon burst, similar to the U.S. housing market in 2005 and 2006.

Readers can be assured that the knowledge-based economy and business transaction environment will not disappear or reverse itself. It's here to stay. Ever-changing and advanced technologies and the intellectual, relationship, and structural capital that a steadily rising percentage of companies globally are comprised of will ensure its longevity.

Any individual who started a career in business prior to the start of the so-called "technology era" (we're now in the "knowledge/intangible asset era") has by now experienced firsthand the very real and significant shift from tangible asset-based economies like manufacturing, to economies and transactions overwhelmingly dominated by intangible assets where proprietary knowledge, know-how, and intellectual capital reign supreme.

Today, it's fair to say, significantly more companies are founded on and underwritten by an idea, bundles of highly specialized expertise, a forward-looking (visionary) capability, and proprietary know-how, each of which are intangible assets!

THERE'S NO BETTER TIME TO ENGAGE YOUR COMPANY'S INTANGIBLE ASSETS

If your company has been adversely affected by this prolonged economic downturn, which it's highly likely it has, there may be no better time or no better use of one's time to take the time to learn more about intangible assets, how to develop them, and the various strategies to exploit them.

This is just one reason why I urge readers to utilize this book as a timely and practical resource to achieve operational familiarity with the still present intangible asset elephant sitting patiently in conference rooms everywhere awaiting action. That is, before electing to pursue a more drastic or less desirable, and quite possibly irreversible, survival-based option that numerous companies have already taken.

Hopefully, but humbly, there is growing evidence that more business operation, legal, accounting, security, and risk management professional communities are on the cusp of more fully engaging their respective responsibilities related to the intangible asset arena. Respectfully, for many, there remains much to learn though, not just from a definitional perspective, but how intangible assets interact and influence a particular industry sector, and its stakeholders, shareholders, and the overall competitiveness of a company, including its market space, and measuring asset performance, relevance, and contributory value.

Now may be the perfect time for management teams to seriously and aggressively delve into the intangible assets their companies are producing or have acquired and figure out how they can best be utilized for both economic and competitive-advantage gains.

Intangible Assets Require Regular Management and Monitoring

When intangible assets are not effectively and consistently managed, overseen, and monitored, they, along with their intellectual-property first cousins, become even more vulnerable to compromise, misappropriation, infringement, counterfeiting, value erosion, and competitive-advantage undermining. This is because conventional forms of intellectual property protection (e.g., patents, trademarks, and copyrights) no longer serve as deterrents or safe harbors, and sophisticated networks of data mining and business/competitor intelligence are increasingly predatorial with their targeting of valuable intangible assets laced with know-how that shortens the distance and resources required to be propelled from a start-up to a thriving global competitor. When these and other risks materialize, the contributory value of a company's intangible assets can, almost instantaneously, go to zero!

It's essential that business management teams globally recognize that, in most every conceivable type of business process, circumstance, or transaction, intangible assets will inevitably be in play and, therefore, at some form of risk. In today's increasingly predatorial, globally competitive, and "winner takes all" business transaction environments, most vulnerabilities left unchecked will inevitably materialize and result in substantial asset value being lost or undermined. This can also create adverse effects to things like reputation and competitive advantages that will cascade throughout an enterprise, affecting its consumers and stakeholders. When this occurs, most companies' sustainability and survivability will be on the line.

Intangible Assets Are Not Theoretical Musings Only to be Embraced in University Lecture Halls

The fact is, intangible assets are permanent and valuable components to most businesses and serve as strong underliers for profitability and sustainability for today, tomorrow, and the foreseeable future!

To readers who start reading this book with a sense of skepticism about intangible assets and the principles and strategies available to help management teams build, safeguard, and deliver value from them, it will be pointed out the value those assets can potentially deliver, the competitive advantages those assets can create, and the threat if those assets are never realized and that they will become diluted, undermined, impaired, or irrevocably lost if they are dismissed or left unengaged and unmanaged.

More specifically, the relevance and contributory value of intangible assets should not be considered as mere theoretical musings or rhetoric more for university lecture halls than management conference rooms. To be sure, the 21st-century's intangible asset–dominated economies and the companies so engaged demand best practices with respect to intangible asset management, oversight, stewardship, and utilization being integral to the repertoire of fiduciary-related tasks and responsibilities already being assumed.

In other words, know-how—that is, intellectual, structural, and relationship capital—represents economic and competitive-advantage power today, but again, only if the holder can effectively safeguard and sustain the necessary control, use, and ownership, and monitor the assets' value, materiality, and risk throughout its respective life cycle. Put simply, the intangible asset elephant cannot and should not continue to be overlooked or dismissed. After all, how can one walk into any conference room no matter how large and not see an elephant?

So, in the chapters that follow, readers will become thoroughly engaged in intangible assets and learn the importance of identifying and aligning them with a company's core mission to build and extract value.

I know from experience, many experienced management team members will find much of the preceding to be the easy part. The hard part is getting intangible assets onto management team radar screens and agendas. So, while some teams may still not consider it a priority or a particularly worthy use of their time right now to pay attention to and act on their intangible assets by learning how to squeeze (i.e., leverage) value from them, this book will hopefully change their mindsets. Engaging a company's intangible assets now may well become an exercise that produces the necessary multipliers and underappreciated or unidentified options for companies to not merely stay afloat, but be profitable, sustainable, and viable for the foreseeable future.

Therefore, please take these perspectives with you while reading this book:

- Intangible assets have become the new "raw materials" for business profitability and success.
- Intangible assets are powerful and valuable assets that management teams need to engage.
- More companies today are being defined by how effectively they manage, deploy, and convert their intangible assets into value and revenue.
- Regardless of a company's size, the nature of its business, its maturity, or its geographic location, all companies produce, possess, and use intangible assets.

- The increasingly competitive global business transaction environment makes identifying, managing, and developing strategies to convert intangible assets into revenue and deliver value and sustainability a critical fiduciary imperative.
- Developing and using intangible assets are business decisions, not solely legal or accounting processes.

Relevant and Forward-Looking Model

I am, first and foremost, an intangible asset strategist, risk specialist, and respectful educator and collaborator on matters related to intangible assets. The proactive perspectives expressed throughout this book collectively form a highly relevant and proactive model for the stewardship, oversight, and management of intangible assets. This is a model in which management teams and other business decision makers, regardless of company size or industry sector, can execute as a starting point to achieve more effective, profitable, and challenge-free transactions whenever and wherever intangible assets are in play.

This book is a culmination of over 25 years of professional consulting, university teaching, continuous research, interactions with hundreds of colleagues and business leaders globally, and publishing on matters related to intangible assets and their close cousin, intellectual property. My consulting engagements, media appearances, and research have focused on identifying, assessing, safeguarding, and managing risk; conducting intangible asset due diligence, and facilitating company transaction cultures designed to enhance intangible assets' contributory value.

In today's world R&D and business transactions are routinely conceived, shaped, and driven by the interconnected flow of data, information, and intellectual capital (intangible assets). This makes it all the more important that the rightful holder of those assets be consistently positioned to realize the full economic and competitive-advantage benefits that the assets are capable of delivering. One requisite for doing this begins by having practices, policies, and procedures in place to sustain control, use, and ownership, and monitor the assets' value, materiality, and risk.

To be purposefully redundant, intangible assets are irreversible and valuable fixtures in most businesses and transactions they routinely engage in.

Global Business Perspective

Throughout the research and writing of this book I endeavored to be consistently conscious that it *not* be conceived solely from a U.S.-based perspective, but rather from a global business perspective. That is because there is truly a global universality to intangible assets, particularly with respect to the requisites for identifying, assessing, valuing, managing, utilizing, exploiting, and safeguarding.

Global universality does not translate however to a one-size-fits-all approach to their stewardship, oversight, and management. Instead, experience clearly conveys that most companies—irrespective of their country registration, industry sector, or boundaryless market space—frequently possess distinctive applications, interconnectedness, and utilization of intangible assets that require nuanced approaches to their management and exploitation to achieve the most effective use, greatest value, and strongest competitive advantages.

To address such nuances, a very practical approach is advocated throughout the book regarding intangible asset management and use, which I respectfully refer to as "what fits best, tends to work best." More specifically, processes, procedures, and practices for developing, nurturing, and exploiting intangible assets that fit best for a company and its culture, will usually work best!

Reluctance, Hesitancy, and Indifference

To management teams and other stakeholders who remain unconvinced, dismissive, or reluctant to engage their company's intangible assets, this book will point out strong rationales for doing so.

While it's true that the global economy is now overwhelmingly derived from intangible assets, it remains, in my view, in its early stages, and some might even say its infancy. There is simply no denying the rising relevance and contributory value of intangible assets. This unforgiving business reality makes it, at best, unwise to characterize intangible assets as merely theoretical rhetoric or new marketing business jargon that will soon fade and give way to other business buzzwords and concepts.

Multitasking, Time-Constrained Readers

Multitasking, time-constrained readers do not have to veer outside their professional domains of expertise to capture and apply the various principles and strategies embedded throughout this book. Instead, this book is designed to build on reader's expertise by adding challenging, relevant, and forward-looking dimensions. And, the book can be read in sequence or by selecting particular chapters that address a current challenge, circumstance, or risk.

In each instance, I am confident readers will learn what intangible assets are and what they aren't, and achieve confidence in identifying, unraveling, assessing, safeguarding, and profitably utilizing intangible assets in a range of professions and (business) transactions. In particular:

- *Corporate suites*: CFOs, CIOs, CROs, CTOs, CMOs, CKOs, CSOs, and IP counsel.

- *Knowledge-intensive, intangible asset-driven companies*: Institutions and organizations engaged in highly competitive and time-/asset-sensitive R&D environments in which intangible assets will inevitably be in play.

- *Professional and personal development*: In disciplines that intangible assets play increasingly significant roles: risk management, marketing, public relations, human resources, sales, financial services, strategic planning, accounting, information assurance, IT security, auditing, accounting, investment banking, venture capital, insurance, due diligence, continuity/contingency planning, and organizational resilience, engineering, security, logistics, serial entrepreneurs, and intellectual property insurance.

- *By job function*: For example, merger and acquisition teams, due diligence teams, business unit heads, project leaders, product developers, systems development, strategic planning, process improvement, and R&D administration.

- *Forward-looking doctoral and graduate students*: Those who recognize the requisites for effectively managing knowledge-intensive businesses and organizations requires the acquisition of strong skills, insights, and operational familiarity with intangible assets.

References

Blair, M., Wallen, S., 1998–2000. Project Co-Directors. Understanding Intangible Sources of Value Research Project (sub-groups). Brookings Institution.

Blair, M., Wallman, S.M.H., 2001. Brookings task force on intangibles. Unseen Wealth: Report of the Brookings Task Force on Intangibles. Brookings Institution Press, Washington, D.C.

IMSDb, Moneyball, screenplay written by Steven Zaillian and Aaron Sorkin, directed by Bennett Miller, retrieved Febuary 28, 2014, Available at <http://www.imsdb.com/scripts/Moneyball.html>.

Chapter 2

Managing
Intangible Assets

The Impetus for Producing Genuine Value

Intangible assets can be the impetus for producing genuine and sustainable value to companies. In most instances, this will only occur when management teams and other decision makers and stakeholders recognize, understand, and set viable strategies in motion to effectively and efficiently utilize their intangible assets.

This entails identifying them, unraveling them, investing in them, positioning them, leveraging them, managing them, and putting best practices in place to sustain their control, use, and ownership, along with monitoring their value and materiality.

Admittedly, there are parts of this book that may require, for some readers, genuine study and reflection. The readers' payoff is understanding the relevance of intangible assets and being able to more confidently and effectively execute the many practical concepts that will unfold throughout.

Above all, I wish to avoid the status quo where many management teams remain dismissive, in the dark, or skeptical about how to identify the intangible assets their company produces; how to value them; how they can be positioned, leveraged, and value extracted; and, perhaps most important, the necessity to protect, preserve control, and monitor the value of those assets (Anston, 2007).

Have You Ever Thought About It This Way?

Why is it that:

■ You can probably pinpoint the precise time of day your desk stapler went missing, but you're absolutely clueless about the status, stability, sustainability, defensibility, and value of your intangible assets, intellectual property, trade secrets, and proprietary know-how and competitive advantages?

■ You will entrust your most valuable intangible assets, business practices, and trade secrets to people or employees you only say hi, goodbye, and thanks to at the office or local copier center?

■ Most companies learn about the value of their misappropriated, compromised, or infringed trade secrets, proprietary know-how, intangible assets, and intellectual property by asking legal counsel what their fees will be to try to get them back?

If you assume that:

■ Your most valuable intangible assets, know-how, and competitive advantages are protected by IT security, nondisclosures, and noncompetes, try listening to cell phone conversations in hotel lobbies and airport lounges, or glance at the laptop screen of the person seated next to you.

■ Your ideas and innovations are adequately protected because a patent has been issued, its time you learned about global data mining, business intelligence, and information-brokering operations, or just go to www.globalfleecemarket.com and see your company's products, ideas, and competitive advantages in counterfeit/pirated form.

■ No one is interested in your strategic planning, client lists, pricing strategies, research, and business practices, why are there more than 19 university programs in the United States and Canada plus hundreds of seminars conducted globally to train people in the art and science of collecting and analyzing business and economic intelligence?

Think about the time, not that many years ago, and the conversations that must have occurred in the R&D laboratories of Toyota when they were conceiving their Prius automobile. I have little doubt at roughly the same time GM and Ford were still thinking about what to name their newest and ever-the-more-larger sport utility vehicle (SUVs) and churning out those SUVs at record paces. By the time GM and Ford woke up and began retooling, redesigning, and laying off thousands of workers, Toyota's Prius brand was well established with commensurate image, goodwill, and loyalty, and now they literally own that market space.

So today is a great time for management teams in all industries to consider "taking a page" from the Toyota Prius playbook and thinking about their equivalent products. In other words, thinking about how their products can produce beneficial intangible assets, i.e., a prius effect.

But still, management teams must ask the right questions, for example:

- Where do our company's intangible assets lie?
- What type of planning is necessary to identify and unravel our company's intangible assets?
- How does our company make money or extract value from its intangible assets?
- Is it really worth our time?
- How long will it take before our company sees evidence of a return from its intangible assets?

For starters, management teams may want to think about it this way: the effective stewardship, oversight, and management of intangible assets can be the difference between looking forward and looking through a rearview mirror. Stewardship, oversight, and management of a company's intangible assets are an investment that can produce revenue and competitive advantages—in other words, "the Prius effect"!

So, if a tree falls in a forest when no one is around, does it make a noise? Similarly, if a company's asset is intangible—that is, it can't be seen or physically touched—how can it tangibly contribute to that company's value, revenue, profits, margins, reputation, image, goodwill, and competitive advantages?

While we clearly know the answer to the first question is yes, the answer to the second question sometimes appears less clear. This chapter will help unravel the answer for readers.

Economist Intelligence Unit Survey

A few years ago, the Economist Intelligence Unit (2003) conducted and published a survey (commissioned by Accenture) in which senior executives from companies around the world were asked to share their views on the management of strategic assets, both tangible and intangible.

Not surprisingly, 94 of the 120 respondents said that "managing intangible assets and/or intellectual capital is an important management issue." Despite that forward-looking testament, a significant majority of the respondents said they "did not have a robust system in place to measure and manage the performance of intangible assets," even though nearly half of the respondents readily acknowledged that the stock market rewarded companies that invest in intangible assets.

In my experience, a healthy starting point to remedy these perplexing survey responses would be to bring more business and economic clarity to intangible assets for global management teams to aid them in recognizing precisely what intangible assets are and what they aren't. They need to be able to identify and distinguish intangible assets and assess their contributory value and competitive advantages they produce.

Two additional and perhaps larger points are worth making. The first is there is an inference embedded in surveys like this that intangible assets remain the province of large, Fortune 500 multinational corporations. There is nothing further from the truth. The reality is intangible assets are literally embedded in most every company, ranging from start-ups, to university-based spin-offs, to SMEs (small, medium enterprises), as well as to mature firms. Intangible assets have little, if virtually nothing, to do with a company's size or industry sector. It's truly not a case of size matters! Rather, it's a matter of management teams being intellectually and operationally clear on what intangible assets are, and actually recognizing what intangible assets their company possesses, produces, and/or has acquired.

Second, most issues today related to or affecting a company's intangible assets have moved from being merely voluntary (we'll do it if we have time) to truly constituting obligations, if not fiduciary responsibilities, for management teams. Either way, intangible assets warrant consistent and well-conceived stewardship, oversight, and management.

Intangible asset management is defined here as consistent stewardship, oversight, and monitoring of the assets to ensure control, use, ownership, and value are sustained indeterminately, but particularly throughout the assets' life, value, and functionality cycles, or otherwise reflect the assets' owner's will.

However, when management teams are dismissive of the economic fact that more than 80% of their company's value, sources of revenue, and sustainability lie in intangible assets and the execution of effective asset management, it's unlikely they will find many sustainable economic benefits, competitive advantages, or efficiencies flowing to their company from these assets.

Responsibilities underlying effective intangible asset management include:

- Identifying and unraveling the origins and development of internally developed assets, as well as those acquired externally.
- Assessing key assets relative to, among other things, their contribution to company value, revenue, competitive advantages, and reputation.
- Ensuring the assets are integrated with the company's core mission and strategic objectives.
- Consistently monitoring the assets to determine if erosion or undermining of their value or competitive advantages has occurred or reputational risk has elevated.

- Ensuring intangible assets are part of routine management discussions to consider ways to make the assets more revenue-value useful, increase their attractivity to investors, leverage the assets to enhance market position, utilize the assets to achieve greater competitive advantages, and create operational efficiencies.

Unfortunately, all too frequently the contributions and competitive advantages intangible assets deliver to a company are overlooked, neglected, or outright dismissed. There are a variety of reasons for this, some already conveyed, but the larger one may well have to do with their lack of physicality, or as I sometimes refer to it the proverbial "can't see the forest for the trees."

That is, while intangible assets are openly and routinely embedded in many company operations, processes, and functions, they are also frequently taken for granted, leaving them unrecognized for their contributory value, and thus they fall under conventional MBA-oriented radar that in many instances still tends to focus on tangible assets.

Achieving operational familiarity with a company's intangible assets will produce numerous multiplier effects for the company along with risk mitigators. Examples include:

- Adding predictability to business transaction outcomes by being positioned to assess factors such as assets' stability, fragility, sustainability, and defensibility that, in turn, elevates the probability for sustaining their control, use, ownership, and value pre- and post-transaction.
- Reducing the vulnerability and criticality to costly, time-consuming, and momentum-stifling legal challenges and disputes through early recognition of circumstances like adverse acts and events that can ensnare or entangle intangible assets in circumstances that impede, erode, or undermine their value, competitive advantages, and overall levels of performance.
- Providing a foundation for more effective use of intangible assets through synergies and efficiencies, particularly knowledge management programs and balanced scorecard approaches, as well as complying with reporting and valuation mandates under Sarbanes-Oxley,[1] FASB 141 and 142, and their European Union equivalents.
- Building a company culture more focused on producing and sustaining intangible assets and providing timely recognition about their use, performance, ownership, materiality, value, and risk.

---

[1] The Sarbanes-Oxley Act (2002) along with new accounting rules adopted by the Financial Accounting Standards Boards require publicly traded companies to measure, monitor, and report the value, materiality, and financial performance of their intellectual property and intangible assets. Under Sarbanes-Oxley, CFO's in particular are charged with making good faith efforts regarding corporate governance through an effective system of enterprise wide internal controls, self-assessments, and operational familiarity with intangible assets.

- Developing more effective business continuity and contingency (organizational resilience) plans by including intangible assets, which paves the way for achieving a quicker recovery of assets following a significant business disruption or natural disaster.

Here are some key best practices and related questions that apply to every company, regardless of size, worth, or industry sector, in terms of managing intangible assets:

- Identify the types and categories of intangible assets that exist in your company as described in Chapter 1.
- Identify, examine, and unravel how those assets evolved—that is, their origins.
- Determine the assets' status—that is, their fragility, stability, durability, sustainability, contributory value, ownership, and risk. It's important to note that the development and use of intangible assets is routinely tied to human capital (i.e., employees).
  - Determine how or if those assets are or are not being utilized or underutilized within the company.
  - Determine specifically how the assets contribute to particular operations, processes, and procedures.
  - Do such linkages contribute to creating and delivering efficiencies, competitive advantages, enhanced customer–client relationships, influencing additional revenue sources, and strengthening the company's reputation?
- Determine how the use of intangible assets within a company is integrated with the company's core strategic mission. In other words, do the intangible assets directly support the company's strategic plan and contribute to enhancing sales of products and services through strong relationship capital?

Under many circumstances, it's appropriate for management teams to communicate their company's intangible asset strategy to employees, along with periodic follow-ups to embed the strategy as an integral component to a company's culture.

For management teams, having an operational familiarity with intangible assets can also deliver favorable multipliers, such as:

- Add predictability to business transaction outcomes when intangible assets are in play by recognizing asset stability, fragility, defensibility, and sustainability.
- Elevate the probability for achieving projected returns, sustaining competitive advantages, and contributing to recognizing asset efficiencies and affirming projected exit strategies.
- Reduce probability of costly and time-consuming legal challenges by recognizing circumstances that can impede, erode, or undermine transaction value, competitive advantages, and projected performance.
- Develop a more comprehensive business continuity and contingency (organizational resilience) plan that encompasses key intangible assets.

The stewardship, oversight, and management of a company's intangible assets should no longer be considered passive or optional responsibilities that occur when there is enough time, when competitors are doing something, or when the government enforces a regulatory mandate.

Neither should those responsibilities be delegated to the uninitiated—that is, those who are dismissive of intangible assets, hesitant to engage them, or convey a nonchalant attitude regarding their use. Managing, overseeing, and stewarding a company's intangible assets need not be extraordinarily time-consuming or resource-intensive undertakings. Rather, what's required upfront is merely being receptive and committed to learning what intangible assets are and how they contribute to a company's value.

Dr. Deming and "All Things Management"

Of all things management attributed to Dr. W. Edward Deming, perhaps one of the most often cited is the adage "You can't manage what you don't measure" (Daines, 2008). As interpreted by most, this adage suggests that unless and until management teams can begin to measure what they're managing, it's unlikely they will know if there's improvement or be able to manage for improvement.

Another lesser-known adage attributed to Dr. Deming is also relevant to the management of intangible assets: "Running a company on visible figures alone constitutes one of the seven deadly diseases of management." Here, Dr. Deming is pointing out that there are many important things in businesses that must be managed, but not all of them can be effectively managed or measured by relying on conventional techniques or methods, particularly those associated with the management and measurement of tangible types of assets (Hunter et al., 2012).

At the time Dr. Deming's adages were originally espoused, intangible assets were hardly on many radar screens in academia or even, it's probably safe to say, among the most forward-looking business management teams in the world. Consequently, it may be doubtful whether Dr. Deming fully appreciated just how relevant the deadly managerial disease of running a company on visible figures alone would ultimately become in the latter third of the 21st century as knowledge-based intangible assets overwhelmingly eclipsed tangible assets as companies' primary source of value and revenue.

As most management teams have come to know in the present intangible asset–dominated global economy, there is no other time in business management and governance history when measuring, managing, and monitoring the value of intangible assets is more necessary or more integral to a company's success.

However, many management teams continue to seek more efficient, objective, and standardized techniques to measure and monitor a company's intangible assets. Also being sought are more objective techniques to identify and assess fluctuations and losses in intangible asset value, along with materiality changes and intangible asset obsolescence.

As techniques evolve and receive confidence from management teams and the relevant regulatory agencies, Dr. Deming's adage to manage what can be measured will be realized, which, among other things, will allow companies to avoid devoting time and resources trying to sustain and preserve once valuable and useful intangible assets that have already experienced measurable losses or obsolescence, or their competitive advantage value has been undermined or significantly devalued!

This does not mean, however, management teams should summarily cast those assets aside for a zero return. Rather, in my view, it means, exploring ways those assets remain valuable and their use could still be leveraged—that is, sell them, barter them, transfer them, license them, hold them, or bundle them, perhaps with other assets, to extract as much value as possible.

Strategic Planning and Intangible Assets

Strategic planning is about communicating a clear, practical, and collaborative vision about where a company wants to be at some point in the future. An actual strategic plan will describe specific action steps necessary to achieve that vision, for example, an assessment of the resources (human, capital, material, etc.) necessary to execute the plan.

Strategic planners would be remiss if they overlooked the contributions intangible assets make to achieving the success planned relative to a company's future. Not factoring the contributions of intangible assets into a strategic plan would leave significant gaps and would hinder, if not totally obfuscate, the work that went into developing the plan.

The importance of factoring intangible assets in strategic planning has been elevated in part because of the emphasis placed on intangible assets in Sarbanes-Oxley and FASB and their international equivalents relative to accounting and reporting the value of intangible assets and any materiality changes.

An increasingly relevant prelude to company strategic planning is to conduct an intangible asset assessment, the primary purpose of which is to bring insight and strategic, business, economic, and competitive advantage clarity to a company's intangible assets. This assessment should:

- Identify relevant intangible assets—that is, their creation, utilization, positioning, leveraging, and ways to extract value.
- Unravel the assets to assess their stability, fragility, and sustainability to ensure control, use, ownership, and value of the intangible assets is sustained relative to the strategic plan's term.

- Put in place practices and procedures to protect the assets' control, use, ownership, and value.
- Assess the assets' contribution to each transaction a company may engage in, such as joint ventures, strategic alliances, mergers, acquisitions, etc.

Identifying and assessing intangible assets by an intangible asset strategist and risk specialist are necessary elements to strategic planning because unlike patents, trademarks, or copyrights, there is no certificate issued by the government that states which intangible assets belong to a company. Also, intangible assets are often embedded, without fanfare or notice, in a company's routine operations, processes, and functions.

While strategic planning is about articulating a clear and practical vision of where a company wants to be at some future point in time, it also describes the necessary action steps for the resources required to execute and achieve the goals and vision of the plan.

Far too often, company strategic planning as far as intangible assets are concerned falls short on two fronts:

- They overlook the role, contributions, and ways intangible assets can be used and leveraged to enable the achievement of the goals, objectives, and vision set forth in the plan.
- They tend to unwittingly focus on a company's tangible assets while overlooking the underlying foundational value and contributions produced by intangible assets, which are likely already embedded in various processes, procedures, and human-intellectual capital.

Still, many strategic planning initiatives tend to see all things tangible by focusing predominantly on a company's external environment. Today, business decision makers would be hard-pressed to argue intangible assets are not relevant to strategic planning.

On the other hand, I do find management teams who are becoming more familiar with and achieving greater confidence in the strategic management and oversight of their company's intangible assets. This includes learning and honing skill sets that lend themselves to identifying and leveraging intangible assets to enhance and extract value and competitive advantage.

However, the ability to execute, advance, and sustain competitive advantages is largely dependent on the foresight and willingness of management teams to ensure that intangible assets remain routine action items on their respective agendas. For example, the necessity to produce ongoing tactical-oriented assessments of a company's intangible assets, and forward-looking and strategic assessments to project what intangible assets should be acquired or nurtured as preludes to creating and underpinning competitive advantages that reflect a company's over-the-horizon strategic planning, product and service trajectories and trends, industry and sector forecasts, and consumer expectations.

Intangible assets left unmanaged, unrecognized, underutilized, or merely dormant will obviously produce few, if any, sustainable competitive advantages or deliver any substantive or lasting value to a company. Doing so will ensure the assets' value will erode and become undermined by competitors or economic adversaries alike.

Strategic and Collaborative Business Decisions

All things intangible, then, should be treated as strategic and collaborative business decisions, many of which can be leveraged as offensive or defensive weapons to guide and advance a company (Reitzig, 2004).

To do this, Dr. Nick Bontis (2002) identified five relatively straightforward steps a company can take:

1. Conduct an initial assessment to identify each intangible asset's status, stability, fragility, value, sustainability, and linkages to producing revenue and competitive advantages.
2. Integrate knowledge and awareness programs about intangible assets throughout the company with linkages to personnel training and evaluations.
3. Integrate best practices to ensure the intangible assets that have been identified as contributing to value and revenue are sustainable—that is, their value, control, use, and ownership are effectively safeguarded and preserved.
4. Develop an internal roadmap describing the company's intangible assets (i.e., producers, location, value, linkages, contributions, and status), and explore strategies for how to better utilize, exploit, and leverage those assets through internal and external collaboration, and align those assets with the company's strategic business plan.
5. Monitor processes related to sustaining control, use, ownership, and value of the intangible assets, and identify gaps and lapses that should be addressed or remedied relative to extracting value.

Anston (2007) consistently emphasizes, as does the Case Business School (UK) in their research, that the value of intangible assets depends on how they are used—that is, their context within a company.

Unlocking Managerial Mysteries to Intangible Assets

There should not be any particular mystery, managerial or otherwise, about best practices for utilizing a company's intangible assets. Yes, there is some specialization that is helpful for identifying and maximizing the value of intangible assets, which comes from intangible asset strategists and risk specialists as discussed earlier.

The key managerial "mysteries" about intangible assets that must be overcome include the reluctance to advocate and develop strategies to measure intangible assets in relatively absolute terms, and the assets' lack of physicality—that is, they cannot be touched or seen in the same manner as physical assets like plants, equipment, and inventory.

To further demystify intangible assets, it's important to recognize and distinguish the three broad categories in which they exist:

- Goods and products of which the value can be established in the marketplace, such as licenses, franchises, patents, trade secrets, and brand value.
- Competencies that include distinctive and sometimes proprietary processes and routines, such as know-how and intellectual capital held and practiced by employees and capable of being created and deployed to the right people at the right time in ways that deliver competitive advantages, value, and bottom-line profits.
- Latent capabilities that include reputation, image, leadership, innovativeness, and the capability of the workforce to create, identify, and respond to market opportunities to accommodate today's hypercompetitive, aggressive, predatorial, and winner-take-all global business transaction environment.

Intangible Asset "Tipping Point"

Published in a conference's proceedings, the Intangible Assets and SME's (2007) presented that a more forward-looking company through more effective stewardship, oversight, management, and reporting of intangible assets carries some degree of risk, most of which can be mitigated while accruing significant business benefits.

Malcom Caldwell (2002) describes three characteristics in his book *The Tipping Point* that I believe are, in many ways, analogous to the current intangible asset phenomena.

The "tipping point," Caldwell says, is merely the "biography of an idea" and the best way to understand the emergence of an idea—in this case, the notion that intangible assets have universally and irreversibly replaced tangible assets as most companies' primary source of value for future wealth creation. Caldwell suggests to think of the transformation as an epidemic. That is, ideas, products, and messages spread in a manner comparable to a virus.

Caldwell describes the "tipping point" as the moment when a critical mass, a threshold, or a boiling point has been reached. With such consistently incontrovertible evidence and economic facts emerging from the global knowledge-based economies that more than 80% of most companies' value and sources of revenue lie in or directly evolve from intangible assets and intellectual property, why hasn't this reality (i.e., the "tipping point" of recognizing intangible assets) become more fully embedded in business strategy? Shouldn't these realities manifest as clear and consistent signs that a critical mass—a "tipping point"—has already been reached and should be exploited?

It's been noted that intangible assets are not the easiest concepts to articulate or apply in business contexts. Those unfamiliar with their existence beyond the single application of goodwill, or are unaccustomed to identifying them and measuring their contribution to a company's value, frequently misperceive intangible assets as representing theoretical concepts best espoused in university lecture halls than in corporate boardrooms.

For management teams and other stakeholders, the "tipping point" for utilizing and exploiting intangible assets has indeed arrived and it's contagious. It's also the reality that oftentimes what begins as small causes can spring forward to have a big effect within companies with positive changes, but perhaps not gradually, but in one dramatic moment!

Intangible Assets: The Hand in Front of Our Faces

All too frequently, as noted many times previously, contributions intangible assets make to a company are overlooked, neglected, or outright dismissed, and sometimes obscured by not knowing precisely where or how intangible assets "fit" on balance sheets and financial statements.

In many, if not most companies, intangible assets are akin to the proverbial "hand in front of our faces." That is, they're often embedded in a company's routine operations, processes, and functions that, in many instances, tend to fall under our radar.

So, why is it beneficial for business unit managers to acquire a familiarity with intangible assets? How will such familiarity produce multiplier effects and risk mitigators while the primary objective is to position and exploit a company's intangible assets to extract as much value and competitive advantage as possible? This objective can be achieved by creating a level of operational familiarity with intangible assets to:

- Add predictability to transaction outcomes by being able to recognize and assess the stability, fragility, sustainability, and defensibility of the assets and their relevance to achieving projected returns, competitive market position, anticipated synergies and efficiencies, and exit strategies.
- Elevate the insightful quality of transaction due diligence by recognizing how to rapidly identify and unravel potentially valuable, revenue-producing assets.
- Reduce the probability that intangible assets will become entangled in costly, time-consuming, and momentum-stifling legal challenges that can erode or undermine asset value, performance, or competitive advantages.

- Contribute to building a company culture that recognizes and is more attuned to intangible assets, their value, and contributions to sustainability and profitability by treating them as business decisions rather than solely legal processes.
- Provide a foundation for more effective application of knowledge management[2] initiatives and balanced scorecard[3] approaches.
- Provide a strong foundation for aligning contingency and risk management planning with strategic business objectives.
- Strengthen the convergence of IT security and intellectual property protection enforcements to achieve more timely awareness of adverse events or acts that in turn permits aggressive pursuit of IP rights violations.

Therefore, ensuring control, use, ownership and value of those assets for the duration of their functional life cycle is the key, in large part due to the assets' increasing relevance to transactions, joint ventures, collaborations, and various other forms of business alliances a company may engage in.

Again, unlike an issued patent, trademark, or copyright, there is no certificate issued by the government that says that the real value of most companies lie in intangible assets other than intellectual properties, such as proprietary know-how, branding, reputation, image, and goodwill.

Intangible Asset and Intellectual Property Values Are Not Static

Intangible asset and intellectual property values are not static! Valuation of those assets should not be measured using one-size fits all, or snapshots-in-time formats. Doing so provides little, if any, strategic post-transaction context to asset values. For the most part, intangible assets tend to be specific to each company and their particular market space. Once any of those assets are compromised or infringed, however, their economic value, along with the market position and competitive advantages they underlie, can begin hemorrhaging immediately, globally, and irretrievably!

---

[2] Knowledge management is a set of practices aimed at discovering and harnessing an organization's intellectual resources, fully utilizing the intellects of the organization's people. Knowledge management is about finding, unlocking, sharing, and altogether capitalizing on the most precious resources of an organization's people's expertise, skills, wisdom, and relationships. Knowledge managers find these human assets, help people collaborate and learn, help people generate new ideas, and harness those ideas into successful innovations. Typically, knowledge management relies on software that lets employees contribute what they know and share that knowledge readily with one another (Bateman and Snell, 2009).

[3] In recent years, a growing number of companies have combined targets for managers into a balanced scorecard, a combination of four sets of performance measures: (1) financial, (2) customer satisfaction, (3) business processes (quality, efficiency), and (4) learning and growth. The goal is generally to broaden management's horizon beyond short-term financial results so the company's long term success is more likely.

Intangible assets and intellectual property are no longer the exclusive beneficiary of conventional IP enforcements or deterrents, largely because the global infringement, misappropriation, counterfeiting, business intelligence, data mining, and economic espionage industries have literally become economically, socially, and culturally embedded in many countries' GDP. To effectively thwart the global market influence of counterfeits and pirated products is a long-term and collective initiative in which companies should not expect to experience a favorably noticeable change for 5–10 years at minimum.

And, once trade secrets are gone, they are probably gone forever. A company's core assets and competitive advantages can be quickly gleaned, analyzed, and applied by sophisticated and predatorial data mining technologies and rapidly growing overnight competitive adversaries like infringers, counterfeiters, and information brokers. However, few intangible assets have the potential to be recaptured, reconceived, reinvested, and, ultimately, rebranded if necessary.

In today's extraordinarily competitive business transaction environments, sustainability does not lie solely in patents and other conventional intellectual property-centric practices and strategies that tend to frame assets in monetary contexts. That is, it's in a company's interest that their intangible assets build value not solely for investors and transactions, but also deliver real, long-term strategic value in the form of multipliers and spillovers that spread throughout a company in the form of tangible and intangible assets.

Another consistent challenge remaining for management teams is recognizing and respecting the notion that ideas produced and executed internally are likely to constitute intangible assets. Instead, intangible assets are routinely and unceremoniously embedded in products and services without fully appreciating their contribution to value, reputation, goodwill, or delivering competitive advantages. Unfortunately, it's still likely those sometimes substantial benefits will go unnoticed, unrespected, or undervalued and, equally important, unprotected!

These are indeed business management realities today that prompt substantive changes in business strategic thinking and operations.

Ten Facts Management Teams Absolutely Need to Remember

1. It's an economic fact that more than 80% of most companies' value and sources of revenue evolve directly from intangible assets, thus these assets will be in play and integral to most transactions.

2. Conventional intellectual property protections issued, such as patents, copyrights, and trademarks, no longer constitute standalone deterrents to or safe harbors from infringers, product counterfeiters, or misappropriation.

3. The value, competitive advantages, and efficiencies produced by intangible assets are often fragile, perishable, and nonrenewable. Once compromised, full asset recovery is seldom achievable.

4. The management, stewardship, and oversight of a company's intangible assets are often characterized as being the primary domain of legal counsel and accounting processes. Such conventional perspectives need to be reframed to include management teams.

5. The timeframe when a company can realize the most value from their intangible assets is relative to an asset's respective functionality life cycle.

6. The growing global universality of regulatory mandates for accounting and reporting the value, materiality, and performance of intangible assets and their international equivalents has led to greater transparency.

7. Intangible assets are increasingly vulnerable to compromise, value erosion, and undermining. Such risks have risen to the point that management teams should assume that once an asset has been compromised, economic and competitive advantage hemorrhaging will start immediately and globally.

8. Many of the risks to intangible assets, such as theft and compromise, are attributed to highly sophisticated and globally predatorial data mining, open-source data analysis, competitive intelligence, and state-sponsored industrial espionage operations.

9. Techniques and strategies should be developed for structuring business transactions to prevent, counter, and mitigate risks to intangible assets that should extend beyond conventional audits or business valuation checklists and be applicable to both pre- and post-transaction contexts.

10. Intangible asset measurement should be less about how to measure and more about determining what assets to measure, which assets carry proprietary elements and competitive advantages, and the interconnectedness of those assets.

Make Intangible Assets Part of the Business Management Lexicon

One of the more frustrating aspects to promoting awareness of intangible assets is the sometimes rather obscure language used to actually define intangible assets.

I, like many of my colleagues, have encountered countless circumstances in which uninitiated management teams, investors, and employees alike, struggle to make sense of intangible assets, or what the British often describe as the invisibles. The British characterization of intangible assets is quite realistic and understandable because, among other things, seldom, if ever, are intangible assets singularly reported on company balance sheets or financial statements, that is, unless they've been acquired or "lumped together" as goodwill.

Still, business decision makers should be hard-pressed to deny the reality that steadily rising numbers of companies have fewer tangible assets in their inventory. Instead, their inventory is being replaced with intangible assets!

A glaring reality is that most every company, not just the new, knowledge-intensive ones, through their management teams and employees, create substantial intellectual, relationship, and structural capital. Whether we're operating a successful business or conducting a scientific project, we tend to seek a comfort zone comprised of facts, figures, formulas, and ratios. In other words, qualitative and quantitative components that with more regularity, constitute the framework for business decisions and strategic planning. Under these circumstances, most business decision makers' comfort zone is fairly easy to sustain because the measurement tools we are accustomed to using and relying on tend to possess tangible characteristics wherein a high number or percentage is interpreted one way and a low number or percentage is interpreted differently.

But sometimes, that comfort zone may be more obscure or fuzzy than we are accustomed to—that is, intangible. In such instances, management teams are challenged to push their conventional understanding and decision-making criteria beyond the tangible to the intangible relative to the relationship and contributory value the latter consistently delivers to companies and organizations globally.

So, welcome to the specialized, but ever-expanding corner of the information age and its outgrowth, the knowledge-based economy, wherein intangible assets now routinely play key roles as contributors to most companies' value, sources of revenue, competitive advantages, sustainability, and building blocks for growth and future wealth creation.

Achieving A More Intangible Asset–Conscious Business Community

Having taught fulltime in universities for more than 20 years, and now owning my own business consulting firm, and literally being in the "trenches" daily spreading the gospel about the importance of intangible assets to management teams representing all business sectors including university technology transfer, I find an important and initial step to achieving a more intangible asset-conscious business community is to bring greater operational clarity about intangible assets, and focus on the benefits that can readily accrue to companies that identify and effectively utilize their intangible assets.

However, I find that even experienced, astute, and successful business management team members seldom utter the words "intangible assets" as part of their routine business lexicon. However, interestingly, through conversations with countless business owners and management team members, I find they can frequently identify a variety of companies, across industry sectors, that have effectively captured and exploited their intangible assets compared to those companies that haven't.

Thus, intangible asset strategists and risk specialists who conduct briefings, awareness training, and consult with companies about their intangible assets should always be prepared to field an array of skeptical, dismissive, and critical questions, particularly with respect to asset valuation and contributory value.

Ironically, in the midst of this extended economic downturn, conventional wisdom would suggest that company management teams would be seeking and be receptive to alternative, yet proven strategies to engage and exploit their company's intangible assets. The bottom line though is, some management teams find it challenging to step outside their conventional comfort zones to engage concepts and strategies that they have not personally tested.

Successful companies are typically run by successful management teams. For the most part, those management teams are realists and pragmatic risk-takers. Therefore, quite understandably, they may express some well-intended skepticism about intangible assets for all the reasons cited in this chapter. However, when such skepticism translates into companies being restrictively tied to practices and strategies of a tangible asset–based economy versus a knowledge-based global economy, they're not likely to experience the growth that they are probably capable of.

References

Anston, W., 2007. The Intangible Asset Handbook: Maximizing Value from Intangible Assets. American Bar Association, Chicago.

Bateman, T.S., Snell, S.A., 2009. Management: Leading and Collaborating in a Competitive World, 8th ed. McGraw-Hill, Irwin, p. 9.

Bontis, N., 2002 March/April. The rising star of the chief knowledge officer. Ivey Business Journal.

Caldwell, M., 2002. The Tipping Point: How Little Things Make a Difference. Little Brown and Company, Boston.

Daines, G. If you can't measure IP, you can't manage IP. Ideanomics Blog. May 15, 2008.

The W. Edwards Deming Institute. <https://deming.org>. McGraw-Hill; 1st edition (November 20, 2012).

Economist Intelligence Unit, 2003. Accenture: Intangible assets and future value.

Hunter, L., Webster, E.M., Wyatt, A., 2012. Accounting for expenditure on intangibles. Abacus 48 (1), 104–145. Available at SSRN: <http://ssrn.com/abstract=2021673>.

Intangible and SME's. Report of the Association of Chartered Certified Accountants. February, 2007. Survey conducted by Dr. Chris Martin commissioned by the ACCA, UK's Department of Trade and Industry, and the Intellectual Property Institute.

Reitzig, M., 2004. Strategic Management of Intellectual Property, MIT Sloan Management Review. Spring.

Chapter 3

Intangible Assets Business Transaction Due Diligence

A New Look at Due Diligence: Focus on Intangible Assets

The due diligence procedures described in this chapter are distinctive in that they focus exclusively on intangible assets. The reason, as repeated throughout this book, is that more than 80% of most companies' value and sources of revenue today either lie in or evolve directly from intangible assets. Any business transaction due diligence team who overlooks or produces dismissive assessments of a target's intangible assets, which are so integral to achieving a desired outcome, truly fall short of their responsibilities to provide decision makers with the highest-quality insight.

Most conventional approaches to due diligence do not comprehensively address intangible assets other than characterizing them in snapshots-in-time value contexts. And, seldom, if ever, do existing due diligence processes provide decision makers with both a current and future context about the status, stability, sustainability, vulnerability, contributory value, and defensibility of intangible assets that are value, revenue, and competitive-advantage components to any merger, acquisition, or asset transfer.

Similarly, most current due diligence practices or protocols seldom, if ever, identify a target's key intangible assets, unravel their origins, or ascertain their contributory value in both pre- and post-transaction contexts. Nor do most conventional due diligence initiatives reveal and then monitor abrupt changes or fluctuations in intangible assets' status, value, and risk exposure. While each has relevance to a transaction's outcome, the materialization of risk has many forms that unfortunately are increasingly frequent and common occurrences in today's businesses. It can be very devastating to transaction-initiating companies to not have an effective "heads up" on these important issues related to intangible assets.

It's important for readers to recognize that today, the value of intangible assets and intellectual property seldom remains constant; rather, it can fluctuate and change, sometimes quite rapidly and for various reasons. Some changes are nefarious, while others are expected consequences to the announcement of a merger or acquisition. Either way, if due diligence management teams are operationally unfamiliar with intangible assets and fail to reveal transaction-relevant characteristics of their contributory value, sustainability, and risk, it can cause an entire transaction to return to the negotiating table.

Intangible asset-focused due diligence services constitute a foundation for building a strong business rationale for management teams to literally reorient their conventional due diligence processes away from the presumption they are primarily legal, accounting, and auditing functions to being more inclusive and collaborative with financial, security, accounting, auditing, and risk management roles and inputs. Also, by making business transaction due diligence management teams more inclusive and collaborative, they will acquire the expertise to conduct their work to accommodate various types of transactions and their company's core business strategies—that is, their products, services, and culture. A due diligence engagement should be collaborative, and not solely a legal, auditing, or accounting task.

Realistically, even though more companies and their management teams have achieved varying levels of familiarity with intangible assets, there still remain many that have not. These firms need to strengthen their operational familiarity with intangible assets as a prelude to formulating and executing strategies to differentiate the intangible assets they produce and how they are embedded as value, revenue, and competitive-advantage contributors for particular products and services. High on this list are intellectual and structural capital.

In this regard, it's essential that management teams have a clear understanding where the value, sources of revenue, competitive advantages, and efficiencies of a target company originate and lie both internally and externally. The answers to these and other equally important questions cannot be found with mere yes or no responses. Rather, each requires a level of investigatory elaboration that can only be achieved by performing a due diligence engagement with strong operational familiarity with intangible assets.

In this chapter, readers will recognize the importance of the following:

■ To quickly reach a consensus on the prioritization of resolution strategies—that is, stop and mitigate further economic hemorrhaging of the assets or elevate criticality.
■ To design and put in place particular safeguards to sustain as much intangible asset value as possible.
■ To achieve the first two tasks through collaboration with intangible asset strategists, intellectual property counsel, accounting, security, risk management, auditing, and compliance.
■ For the strategy to reflect the company's preferences, needs, and resources relative to trying to reestablish asset value and competitive advantages, and reobtain control of the contested assets.

Business Transaction Due Diligence

Experienced business persons would be hard pressed not to assume intangible assets will invariably be in play in most every conceivable type of business transaction today. Therefore, to exclude intangible assets from any transaction would be a significant error that would, in all likelihood, pave the way for a less-than-desirable outcome for the transaction as a whole.

Most business transactions are aggressive, often negotiated in a "winner takes all" manner. Coupled with that characterization are the asymmetric risks and threats that are consistently present. Properly conducted intangible asset-directed due diligence can mitigate, if not remedy, these risks. However, it must be recognized that such risks, when they materialize, can stifle a transaction's momentum, undermine investors' enthusiasm, and weaken confidence in achieving a profitable exit strategy by eroding newly projected returns, and ultimately change the entire complexion of the transaction. At least with a strong intangible asset due diligence, the principals would have been given a proper warning. So, if the intangible assets' risks were high, the principals' would have the option to cancel the deal, or return to the negotiating table with evidence to seek and probably receive more favorable terms.

The Primary Objective

The primary objective for any due diligence undertaking when intangible assets are in play is to provide superior and relevant knowledge to the principals and alert them to the status, stability, sustainability, and risks to the about-to-be-purchased intangible assets. This involves revealing, among other things, the following:

■ Overconfident or embellished representations.
■ Premature disclosures, open-source leaks, or asset compromises.

■ Entanglements, challenges, or disputes that the assets may have already succumbed to internally or externally.

■ Conducting a business impact analysis relative to any of these risks, but also including business intelligence and economic espionage initiatives.

Importantly, business transaction due diligence, with its focus on intangible assets, should go well beyond a conventional checklist mentality. Conventional checklist types of due diligence seldom provide the principals with insights for assessing whether the intangible assets are properly positioned and safeguarded to sustain the deal's terms, objectives, projected financial interests, and returns, or cause undue friction that can delay deal closure. Any one of the risks mentioned here can undermine an investment.

Learning all relevant information about a targeted business should be the primary objective of the due diligence team and process. Due diligence activities are iterative—that is, additional information may produce the need to investigate further for clarification, or determine other avenues of inquiry are necessary, particularly those involving a company's key sources of value, revenue, and competitive advantage—its intangibles (Mergers & Acquisitions Committee, ABA Business Law Section, 2007).

Savvy due diligence team members who understand the nuances of intangible assets are essential contributors. They can identify, unravel, distinguish, and assess intangible assets in a comprehensive and efficient manner that will send a strong message to a target's principals, legal representatives, auditors, and valuators.

Acquiring the Real Picture of A Company's Financial Health

An often overlooked or dismissed requisite to acquiring a complete picture of a company's value, competitive advantages, and financial health is by not closely examining or assessing the intangible assets a company produces and possesses. As readers know, balance sheets and financial statements are portrayed as the primary, sometimes sole, descriptor of a company's financial health and well-being. Balance sheets and financial statements constitute a quick sound-bite of a company's assets and liabilities, along with describing equity positions of owners or stockholders.

Due diligence today must be far more than a mere review of publicly filed documents. After all, intangible assets are seldom, if ever, reported on publicly filed balance sheets or financial statements.

There are three irreversible economic facts and business realities that make it important to disclose the value of intangible assets on financial statements:

1. Intangible assets are just that, intangible. Translated, this means intangible assets are not subject to the five (physiological) senses of touch, smell, hearing,

sight, or taste as tangible assets are, but intangible assets are relevant and valuable assets that take many forms, such as reputation, competitive advantages, intellectual property, branding, etc.

2. A growing percentage of businesses, irrespective of size or sector, operate in a knowledge-based global economy in which more than 80% of their value, sources of revenue, and the building blocks of their growth, sustainability, and profitability evolve directly from intangible assets.

3. Examining a company's balance sheets and financial statements alone, particularly those that do not report intangible assets, and expect to provide principals with a sufficiently comprehensive picture of a company's real financial health, is misleading because knowledge of intangible assets' quality, positioning, and contributory value are critical to making sustainable and lucrative business decisions!

Craig Woodman (n.d.) points out that, in practice, a company's balance sheet is usually formatted with assets at the top, then liabilities, followed by owner's equity. Woodman notes that accounting rules stipulate that, on balance sheets, assets are differentiated as:

- *Current assets* are business assets that are the most liquid. This means they can be readily converted to cash, typically within one year. Examples of current assets are cash and accounts receivable, both of which fund the day-to-day operations of a business.
- *Fixed assets* are physical assets and are typically less liquid—that is, they take longer to convert to cash. Examples of fixed assets are real estate or equipment.

Interestingly, Woodman considers intangible assets as being fixed assets, because he claims they are difficult to convert to cash.

To Woodman's credit, I agree that any business management team who genuinely wants to know the real economic health of their company are obliged to assess the contributory value of their intangible assets. However, in my opinion, it is not that difficult to determine the value of intangible assets, providing one understands and can effectively unravel and track their contributory value.

For example, if I was inclined to purchase a preowned or otherwise used automobile, my decision to buy or not would be only partially price-based. The presence of my targeted auto's maintenance record would provide some evidence whether the previous owner had the motor oil changed at prescribed intervals and performed other maintenance as suggested in the owner's manual. So, a wiser buyer, in my view, should look for and investigate the countless intangible assets related to a vehicle's operation, care, and maintenance that can favorably or adversely impact a vehicle's life cycle and reliability without incurring extensive and expensive repairs.

Again, intangible assets are things that a business produces, possesses, and delivers, preferably in the form of value, revenue, and competitive advantages. However, they have no conventional physical features. In due diligence contexts, all key intangible assets should be unraveled, assessed, and accounted for. In other words, intangible assets are comparable to the purchase of a preowned automobile, in which a buyer presumably calculates the benefits that may be realized because of a lower purchase price. However, absent a comprehensive investigation of a vehicle's maintenance record, a buyer may experience frustrating and expensive repairs that not only minimizes the owner's sense of reliability, but may also cause the buyer to wonder if their decision to buy was not just hasty, but totally wrong.

Intellectual property audits, for example, are intended to ascertain the legal status and defensibility of a company's patents, trademarks, copyrights, etc. If an intellectual property auditor, usually conducted by an attorney, is sufficiently experienced and so inclined, the audit may also include looking for evidence of misappropriation, infringement, compromise, asset devaluation, undermining, or erosion. Most conventional approaches to conducting intellectual property audits resemble snapshots-in-time descriptions of a specific asset's status. In other words, conventional intellectual property audits are time bound and do not reflect or project an asset's vulnerability to asymmetric risks and the real probability of the materialization of risks that will cause adverse circumstances.

Highly Proactive Approach to Due Diligence

Company strategies to safeguard, sustain, and monitor the value of intangible assets must recognize these global business realities:

- There is a constant stream of new players entering the business trade and transaction arena, and some are doing so legacy free—that is, absent any particular bond, allegiance, or respect for conventional intellectual property rights.
- Increasingly sophisticated and predatorial data mining technologies can instantaneously capture and analyze innovation at increasingly earlier stages of its development.

MITIGATE POTENTIAL FOR PROBLEMS, DISPUTES, AND CHALLENGES BY CONDUCTING AN INTANGIBLE ASSET-FOCUSED DUE DILIGENCE AND BUSINESS IMPACT–CRITICALITY ANALYSIS

An initial step to favorably position a company's intangible assets and proprietary competitive advantages and intellectual property in a transaction is to conduct due diligence that incorporates a business impact–criticality analysis. *Criticality* is defined here in the context of a company experiencing a negative event or act and determining the impact it will have on the company's ability to continue to function and return to a state of operational normalcy within a reasonable time period. A return to operational normalcy would, in most instances, be dependent on its ability to actually recover its competitive advantages, reputation, and intellectual, structural, and relationship capital.

An intangible asset-focused due diligence becomes a thorough, systematic, and company-specific process to determine the status, stability, defensibility, value, vulnerability, and recoverability of the intangible assets that were adversely affected by a negative event or act. The ravages of Hurricane Katrina in New Orleans and along Mississippi's coastline along with Hurricane Sandy's devastation of New Jersey's coastline and lower Manhattan and surrounding boroughs are relevant examples. In both of these incidents, there was significant loss of physical assets (i.e., life and property), but the intangible assets related to human resiliency of people desiring to return to those devastated areas to rebuild or vacation are also critical.

I recall giving numerous talks about intangible assets in the months following Hurricane Katrina. I would respectfully describe New Orleans being noted for its food, restaurants, the gayety of the French Quarter, the trolley line, the river walk, the lower ninth ward, and, of course, the accompanying culture, most of which received significant damage or total devastation. Again, the physical damages, loss of life, and horrid conditions thousands of residents had to endure for months, coupled with the rapid migration of residents elsewhere, appeared at times to be assets that would be forever lost. However, the resiliency of the city to recover, obviously with much aid and assistance, laid the foundation for the important and attractive intangible assets to return to the point that New Orleans, with notable exceptions, has reattained operational normalcy.

So, in addition to identifying and assessing elements of company resiliency, a key purpose of integrating a business impact–criticality analysis exercise as a part of an intangible asset-focused due diligence engagement is to ensure the principals receive comprehensive information and insight regarding the intangible assets of resiliency. The business impact–criticality analysis achieves this by distinguishing those intangible assets that can sustain the projected objectives, returns, and exit strategy under particularly extreme circumstances in which misappropriation, business intelligence, infringement, compromise, counterfeiting, and other risks are likely to materialize, sometimes very rapidly and simultaneously.

Important starting points for determining this higher level of intangible asset due diligence include the following:

- Sift through and unravel a company's operational intellectual, relationship, and structural capital and other relevant intangible assets and put in place, as needed, practices to sustain control, use, and ownership, and monitor asset value, materiality, and risk.

- Identify risks and vulnerabilities to key valuable intangible assets that, when incurring risk, can entangle the assets as preludes to costly, time-consuming, and momentum-stifling legal disputes or challenges.
- Identify internal clusters of intangible assets and competitive advantages and assess their contributory current and future value and the adequacy of safeguards to sustain that value when certain risks materialize.
- Alert management teams to vulnerabilities in asset safeguards and value preservation that warrant attention prior to a transaction closure.
- Bring operational and economic clarity to the targets' management teams regarding the intangible assets, company culture, and competitive advantages integral to a transaction's desired outcome.
- Identify effective asset safeguards and value-preservation measures that reflect a transaction's rationale and are aligned with the buyer's strategic business plan, deal objectives, projected returns, exit strategy, and life cycle of the assets themselves.

QUESTIONS THAT MUST BE ADDRESSED PRIOR TO DEAL CLOSURE

During the early stages of negotiating any business transaction in which intangible assets are in play, the due diligence team should address the following questions, which are not presented in any particular sequence. The questions do, however, incorporate a range of circumstances, sectors, products, and services. Intangible asset-focused due diligence teams are encouraged to not accept any question as it stands; rather they should consider the necessity for and ways that a question could be reframed to address nuances of specific engagements or circumstances.

1. What is the company's threshold for asset loss of its competitive advantages and other intangible assets?
2. How quickly (days, weeks, months, etc.) will the company "feel" a materialized risk as an economic or competitive advantage loss, affecting its intangible assets?
3. What, if any, will the degree of breadth or permanency of loss be if key intangible assets are misappropriated, infringed, or counterfeited relative to the costs of trying to recover them reasonably intact and rebuild stakeholder and consumer image, goodwill, reputation, and trust?
4. Which, if any, specific elements of a company's intangible assets exist in open sources or purchased off-the shelf?
5. What is the degree of global universality of the company's services, products, systems, or component parts? That is, do the products and services and the contributing intangible assets have alternative applications? If so, what is required for their adaptability? Are there any known dual-use (e.g., civilian, defense) aspects?

6. Are there particular barriers or requisites to product launches by infringers or counterfeiters to produce, distribute, and sell any counterfeited company products or services, whole or in part? That is, do initial investment, special facilities, equipment, technologies, skill levels, or supply of workers compete with other counterfeiters?

   a. Will counterfeiters require specific access to or theft of proprietary know-how, a photograph of a prototype, or merely the legitimate purchase of an authentic version for reverse engineering?

   b. What, if any, is the degree of deception that needs to be built into a counterfeited product to accommodate regulatory oversight without adversely affecting consumer confidence in or demand for the product?

   c. Do infringers merely need to produce a reasonable look alike or an exact replica?

   d. Are there levels of consumer tolerance or expectations of quality required in a counterfeited product?

   e. Is the craftsmanship of counterfeits transparent/ Can consumers make adjustments to the counterfeited product to elevate its appearance of authenticity?

7. What is the ease and speed with which counterfeits can be distributed and legitimately enter consumer supply chains?

8. What is the cultural (e.g., business, legal, government) tolerance regarding infringement and counterfeiting in a host country where a company's business transactions will occur?

   a. What is the overall importance attached to intellectual property rights in the host country?

   b. Do intellectual property laws in a host country carry inconsequential penalties?

   c. Does a political will exist in the host country to aggressively and consistently enforce intellectual property rights and aggressively pursue infringers and counterfeiters?

   d. Are there statutory requirements in the host country that impede investigation or enforcement of intellectual property rights violations—that is, a particularly cumbersome, time-consuming, or costly process?

   e. If extreme counterfeiting conditions occur in a host country, what is the company's tipping point? Will it be prudent to have a rapid country exit strategy in place?

   f. Will the company be able to build other competitive advantages in the host country, globally, regionally, and in the United States?

9. Do contractual, statutory, and regulatory requisites exist in the host country's intellectual property law and its administration that affect the speed, completeness, and length of time it will take to fully execute a country exit strategy, resulting in additional economic losses?

10. How are existing global levels of counterfeiting affecting the company now in terms of operating capacity, manufacturing costs, pricing, sales, revenues, margins, and demand by consumers?

11. If large-scale counterfeiting does occur, what, if any, affect will this have on the company's material value of intangible assets?

    a. What actions will be necessary to correct the breach and how much will the remediation cost?

    b. Will the fact that a publicly traded company must report the value of its intangible assets cause any changes relative to its legal standing to bring a civil or criminal action?

If a transaction or due diligence team overlooks or dismisses a company's intangible assets, like those embedded in each of the preceding questions, it's tantamount to excluding precisely how and where value, sources of revenue, and sustainability originate or will be created. Thus, if the due diligence management team is dismissive of intangibles that are effectively underwriting a transaction, it's fair to say it's time to either change the composition of the team and quickly engage them in relevant training to achieve the necessary level of operational familiarity with intangible assets.

Benefits of An Intangible Asset Strategist

As readers know, there is an abundance of research that consistently paints very compelling pictures about mergers, acquisitions, strategic alliances, or other types of transactions faltering or failing. I am confident that in most such instances, evidence of potential or impending challenges could have surfaced through effective intangible asset-focused due diligence. Therefore, the benefits of having an intangible asset strategist include the following responsibilities:

- Develop and execute strategic plans to monitor internal and external asset risks and fluctuations in asset value, materiality, impairments, and functionality cycle.
- Add predictability to business transaction outcomes, projected returns, and exit strategies when intangibles are in play.
- Monitor and assess asset stability, fragility, defensibility, and vulnerabilities.
- Conduct market entry planning (due diligence) in both pre- and post-transaction contexts.
- Reduce the probability that project/deal momentum will be stifled by recognizing and mitigating risks.
- Execute comprehensive organizational resilience plans that specifically encompass intangible assets.
- Monitor linkages between the production, acquisition, and utilization of intangible assets relative to their contributions to company value, sources of revenue,

and creating and sustaining competitive advantages, as well as the overall company mission.

■ Provide respectful guidance to business units and management teams regarding effective stewardship, oversight, and management of intangible assets.

Seldom, if ever, given the comprehensive, global-reaching, and technologically sophisticated platforms available today, should risk or challenges come as a surprise. Effective intangible asset-focused due diligence should reveal the presence of potentially adverse circumstances, attitudes, or financials that many times are rooted in the mishandling or disregard for the contributory value of one or more key intangible assets, particularly intellectual, relationship, or structural capital, and reputation.

One technique to mitigate or remedy the probability that a business transaction or project will fail is for decision makers to demand and receive an objective "heads up" from their due diligence team. This is usually best addressed in the form of what has already been described as an intangible asset–impact criticality analysis and should certainly be delivered in sufficient time—that is, in advance of consummating a transaction—so modifications, if necessary, can be fully considered, including terminating a transaction altogether.

As noted, this higher and specialized level of analysis will bring clarity and transparency to transaction proposals with a more definitive and authoritative assessment of the stability, defensibility, sustainability, and contributory value of key intangible assets identified as being essential to transaction success.

The most usable business-impact criticality analysis should include the following:

■ The findings about whether key intangible assets are impaired in some manner—that is, are found to have already been compromised, misappropriated, infringed, counterfeited, or otherwise devalued—and if further impairment can be mitigated or stopped.

■ The probability for the materialization of specific risks that can adversely affect the projected economics, competitive advantages, or projected synergies of a transaction.

■ The strategies for mitigating and containing certain risks relative to the resiliency and sustainability of key intangible assets.

The reason I am an advocate of conducting impact criticality analysis for key intangible assets is because their contributory value is increasingly challenging to sustain throughout the value cycle of the asset. This is due, in no small part, to their mobility and the fact their proprietary status is beholden to various behavioral factors, personal allegiances, and proclivity to inadvertently or purposefully divulge such information.

However, the ultimate objective remains the same: to enable a more secure, profitable, and sustainable transaction going forward.

Costly, Time-Consuming, and Sometimes Irreversible Risks, Challenges, and Disputes

The myriad of asymmetric risks to intangible assets has evolved over the last decade from being relegated to subjective prognostications (i.e., they may or may not materialize), to inevitabilities, particularly when they remain unrecognized, are ineffectively managed or dismissed, or when those responsible for their prevention and mitigation have little or no operational familiarity with intangible assets.

At minimum, there are five ways in which a company's key intangible assets become entangled in costly, time-consuming, and sometimes irreversible legal challenges. Frequently, I find that when intellectual, structural, or relationship intangible assets are at the center of a dispute or challenge, it is frequently a consequence or combination of the following:

- Misplaced or a violated trust among business partners, research collaborators, management team members, or a collusive employee.
- Ineffective asset safeguards or risk mitigation, either of which create vulnerabilities that lead to breaches, compromises, or theft.
- Unethical or illegal conduct of insiders (e.g., employees, contractors, vendors) anywhere within a company's supply chain who exploit opportunities to compromise assets or undermine their value and competitive advantage.
- Management teams' and legal counsels' out-of-touch presumptions that conventional intellectual property enforcements, particularly patents, remain sufficient stand-alone deterrents to economic adversaries along with a disregard for the speed in which asset value and competitive advantages can be compromised and applied to competing or counterfeited products or services.

Characterizing any of these as merely constituting an additional, but minimal risk of doing business in an intangible asset-dominated global economy will lay a foundation for both businesses and the various transactions a company engages in to fall short of expectations or experience complete failure.

Intangible Asset Strategist Risk Officers

Intangible asset strategist risk officers are the new business transaction and due diligence analysts. The principle foundation to the stewardship, oversight, and management of any company's intangible assets lies with management team recognition that practices (policies, procedures, etc.) must be in place to safeguard and sustain control, use, and ownership, and monitor the value, materiality, and risk to key assets.

While I am not always an advocate of assigning priorities to these responsibilities, it is clear that should a particular responsibility be dismissed, overlooked, or neglected, the probability that business intangible asset hazards and risks will materialize rises substantially. And, when particularly carnivorous risks materialize, little else may matter to the victim business because their intangible assets and the value, sources of revenue, and competitive advantages they have produced will likely erode and rapidly go to zero.

With the global business trade and transaction asset risk environment being increasingly dominated by insiders, state actors, legacy free players, and sophisticated business-economic intelligence apparatus, they have collectively become significant and embedded layers of asset risk that most businesses must contend with. For example, the compromise of a key intangible asset can set in motion adverse and unrecallable reputation risks that rapidly cascade throughout an enterprise and among its stakeholders, stockholders, and consumer networks. So, when management and due diligence teams continue to express hesitancy, reluctance, or, worse, a sense of invincibility or resilience about experiencing intangible asset risks and hazards, it's important they be reminded that more than 80% of their company's and most target's value and sources of revenue either lie in or evolve directly from intangible assets!

Thus, as should be evident at this point, when intangible asset risks materialize, having an intangible asset strategist and risk specialist available is not merely worth considering, it may well be a fiduciary responsibility. There should be little argument then that having an intangible asset strategist on board with operational familiarity to thwart or mitigate the ever-expanding array of risks would bring a measurable return-on-security investment to a company.

An effective argument could be made that intangible asset strategists and risk specialists today are equivalent to Wall Street's industry sector analysts who assess and monitor relevant and key variables like market trends, events, cycles, and risks affecting intellectual and structural capital, innovation pipelines, and other intangible assets relative to their short- and long-term sustainability, fragility, or volatility. That's particularly true as intangible assets become more recognizable, migrate into the business lexicon, and continue to play integral roles in all business initiatives and transactions,

Unwarranted Sense of Urgency Should Not Dominate Intangible Asset Strategists' Due Diligence Methodologies

As noted routinely, intangible assets are increasingly valuable commodities the content of which can be developed, nurtured, and leveraged in ways to position management teams to pursue a broader range of transactions or strategic alliances in which intangible assets can be bought, sold, transferred, traded, assimilated, or licensed, as well as having relevance to structuring transactions at the outset and negotiating pricing.

However, these assets can, as routinely noted, become vulnerable to various forms of value erosion, undermining, and competitive advantage hemorrhaging that will impair their ability to produce expected value, revenue, and sustainability that they otherwise would be capable of.

This makes it more essential for transaction management teams to exercise prudence by not succumbing to an unwarranted sense of urgency with respect to consummating any particular business transaction. This includes acknowledging the probability that, at some level, asset hemorrhaging can occur in either pre- or post-transaction contexts. In fact, in some instances, asset hemorrhaging will commence before the ink dries on a transaction contract.

One key to mitigating, if not preventing, some types of pre- and post-transaction asset hemorrhaging is to avoid permitting any unwarranted sense of urgency to adversely affect the thoroughness of the transaction's intangible asset due diligence. When due diligence teams unnecessarily frame a transaction through a lens of urgency and speed, one consequence is that there will be an inclination to use conventional, one-size-fits-all types of instruments that hardly reflect the intensity and role intangible assets routinely play in today's business transactions. In other words, key intangible assets may be overlooked and their sustainability not factored in, nor the number of risks that will inevitably surface.

In addition, in today's "go fast, go hard, go global" business transaction environment, it's quite likely, with respect to any transaction, that there may well be multiple and simultaneous players engaged in parallel transactions that obviously can contribute to a sense of urgency to consummate a transaction without consistently ensuring each of the key intangible assets have been properly and effectively vetted.

In these circumstances, intangible asset hemorrhaging is facilitated by unnecessary sense of urgency attached to transaction consummation. Urgency and speed often mutate as the primary drivers of a transaction, which in turn minimizes the thoroughness of the due diligence, especially with respect to unraveling embedded intangible assets that inevitably will be important components. The assumption is that transactions can be consummated and revenue streams commence before the intangible assets in play fall prey to theft, misappropriation, or simply walk out the front door as intellectual capital (know-how) with departing employees.

Due diligence and transaction management teams, along with their intangible asset strategist counterpart, are obliged to structure and execute their respective roles in a collaborative and complimentary manner that:

- Recognizes the necessity to retain control, use, ownership, and monitor the value, materiality, and risk to the key intangible assets essential to negotiating and achieving a profitable and sustainable transaction outcome.

- Reveals and unravels risks and challenges to key intangible assets that could jeopardize a transaction's success during either the negotiation phase or post-transaction.
- Reduces the probability that risks to intangible assets will materialize to impairment significance by keeping management teams fully apprised of any events and behaviors that will undermine assets' value, competitive advantages, and the ability to continue producing revenue.

Again, the presence of an intangible asset strategist and risk specialist will enable more secure, profitable, and sustainable transactions as they were initially conceived and desired. It is only prudent then to ensure experienced professionals with these specializations are consistently at the transaction table.

With such significant percentages of transaction value now evolving directly from intangible assets, effective due diligence is essential to transaction outcomes. However, it must be much more than a cursory or confirmatory review of the assets' presence, absence, or positioning. Due diligence must provide decision makers with much more than subjective, snapshots-in-time estimates of asset value.

This, of course, is why it's important to examine other important features of intangible assets as part of a due diligence framework, such as their fragility, stability, defensibility, risk, sustainability, and contributory value. Understanding how these characteristics can, and frequently do, interact to affect a transaction's outcome favorably or adversely is relevant insight and context decision makers and transaction management teams should have at the ready. When any one of these characteristics materializes adversely, asset value and utility can be undermined, compromised, or misappropriated very rapidly.

Pre- and Post-Transaction Due Diligence and Asset Monitoring Are Essential to Success

For acquisition management and due diligence teams, the prospect of acquiring intangible assets with contributory value that can be quickly converted or applied to advance a near-term business strategy, should be recognized at the outset as essential elements to achieving the projected benefits of an acquisition. However, acquisition management and due diligence teams must also recognize that a successful acquisition ends at the point in which a target's assets have been legally acquired.

It's important for decision makers and management teams to recognize that merely because a prospective deal or transaction has progressed to the due diligence stage, there is no guarantee the projected values, synergies, and competitive advantages the targeted assets are projected to deliver are sustainable or will be there after the deal has been consummated.

Therefore, the management of acquisition due diligence should be structured to include pre- and post-transaction components:

1. Unravel and assess each of the key assets' status—that is, their stability, fragility, defensibility, and transferability.
2. Continuously monitor those key assets' value and materiality throughout the acquisition process.
3. Put in place measures to ensure the acquiring firm can sustain unchallenged control, use, and ownership, and value of the assets, post-transaction.

The following represents a sampling of questions that should be on every due diligence teams' radar, any one of which is a signal regarding a transaction's success. Is there evidence of:

- A culture that recognizes the value of the core revenue-producing intangible assets?
- Consistent stewardship, oversight, and management of those intangible assets?
- Consistency in the representation of those assets in which risk, value, materiality, and performance are measured?
- Business contingency planning that includes core intangible assets?
- Strategic internal planning that recognizes and utilizes intangible assets as sources of value, revenue, and building blocks for growth, profitability, and sustainability?

Responsibilities for any Due Diligence Team

The following are the responsibilities for any due diligence team:

- Unravel each asset to verify its origins and ownership, and determine if any problematic legal restrictions or liabilities exist that would inhibit unrestricted utilization and commercialization, undermine the asset's value and competitive advantages, or require post-transaction costs to resolve claims or engage in litigation.

- Identify and assess the existence of any circumstances in which the assets are at risk of value erosion, competitive advantage undermining, etc., if a competitor or economic adversary was able to illicitly acquire sufficient intellectual and structural capital to launch a competing comparable product or technology that would render those assets either commercially obsolete or unattractive to consumers and thus shorten the assets' projected life, value, and functionality cycles.

- Determine if any component of the about-to-be acquired assets have already been or will be exported that would trigger additional legal or regulatory compliance requisites that would cause delays, additional costs, inhibit international filings, or preclude export altogether.

■ Determine if significant asset compromises have already occurred that exceed the acquiring party's risk threshold.

■ Determine if key intellectual, structural, or relationship capital is leaving the company in advance of the transaction, and if so, at what level, and how would this adversely impact projections of near-term viability and profitability of the transaction (Files, 2007).

References

Files, L.B., 2010. Due Diligence for the Financial Professional. Aegis Journal, 2nd Edition. Tempe, AZ.

Mergers & Acquisitions Committee, ABA Business Law Section, 2007. International Mergers and Acquisitions Due Diligence. American Bar Association, Chicago.

Woodman, C. What Is The Difference Between A Balance Sheet and Cash Flow Statements. Chron. Small Business by Demand Media. No date. Year Unknown; Accessed 2014.

Chapter 4

New Dimensions for Company Management[1]

Most intellectual property safeguards and enforcement initiatives (e.g., patents, copyrights, and trademarks) are more reactive than proactive. To be effective, intellectual property holders must be alerted in a timely manner, almost in real time, to the materialization of harmful, value-depleting, competitive advantage-eroding risks, including theft, infringement, and misappropriation. Absent implementing precautionary measures—that is, putting in place effective safeguards to inhibit, prevent, and mitigate risks to intangible assets—when certain risks do materialize, the consequences can be irreversible.

---

[1] The inspiration for this chapter was sparked by "Allegiance in a Time of Globalization" (Defense Personnel Security Research Center, Technical Report 08–10, Dec. 2008); "Technological, Social, and Economic Trends That Are Increasing U.S. Vulnerability to Insider Espionage" (Defense Personnel Security Research Center, L. A. Kramer, R. J. Heuer, Jr., K. S. Crawford, Technical Report 05–10, May 2005); and America's Increased Vulnerability to Insider Espionage, *International Journal of Intelligence and Counterintelligence* 20 (2007): 50–64.

For intangible asset-dependent firms, it's critical for safeguards to be significantly more proactive in their design and implementation to rapidly assess and mitigate risks. Steps toward mitigation start with the following:

- Recognizing the necessity to anticipate, assess, and secure the resources necessary to counter and mitigate risks, but preferably prevent risks to intangible assets from materializing in the first place.
- Differentiating general and specific types of deterrents. For most, deterrents are presumed to be naturally occurring outcomes of security systems, products, and services—that is, a vast majority of people will be deterred from engaging in illegal acts merely by the presence of a policy or law. But with increasing frequency and technological sophistication in today's business world, risks routinely materialize and can rapidly cascade throughout a company.

This model is particularly relevant to intangible asset-dependent companies due to the adverse economic effects following asset losses, compromises, and reputation risk, any of which can be immediate, costly, long lasting, and frequently irreversible. Gerald Ratner, the U.K. retail tycoon, following the demise of his £500M jewelry business is reported to have said, Intangible assets take years to build and a second to lose!

Therefore, highly proactive practices designed to sustain control, use, and ownership, and routinely monitor the value and materiality of a company's intangible assets, should be routine action items on management team agendas. They should also become priorities for chief security officers (CSOs), intellectual property counsel, chief risk officers (CROs), chief intellectual property officers (CIPOs), and chief financial officers (CFOs). That is because intangible assets are integral to not just a company's value, but its competitiveness, sources of revenue, investment potential, market position, and overall value.

Most management teams recognize there has been a significant shift in the origins of company value and revenue from tangible to intangible assets. While there is no precise year when this shift started, it was initially recognized in the early to mid-1980s as constituting a key springboard into a global knowledge-based economy.

This shift warrants more proactive and aggressive safeguards, risk management techniques, and legal counsel oversight. However, because intangible assets are nonphysical, designing consistently effective safeguards presents challenges for those unfamiliar with the intricacies of intangible assets, aside from conventional forms of intellectual property.

This shift makes it necessary for CFOs, CSOs, CIPOs, and CROs to acquire operational familiarity with their company's intangible assets:

- What they are and are not.
- How they develop and evolve to create contributory value, sources of revenue, and competitive advantages.
- Their nuanced, sophisticated, and asymmetric risks.

- The various ways risks can materialize to adversely affect their economics.
- To execute effective practices to protect the control, use, and ownership, and monitor value, materiality, and risk to the key intangible assets.

Safeguarding Intangible Assets Throughout Their Life Cycles

By now readers know that it is an irreversible economic fact that more than 80% of most companies' value, sources of revenue, and building blocks for growth, profitability, and sustainability globally evolve directly from intangible assets!

However, companies are essentially on their own to find the requisite services and expertise to understand intangible assets and their respective contributory values. Also, such services and expertise are rapidly becoming fiduciary responsibilities that fall exclusively to management teams to articulate and execute as a foundation to gain and sustain asset value and competitive advantages efficiently, effectively, and consistently.

More specifically, the actual and contributory value of many, if not most, intangible assets fluctuates, sometimes in cyclic fashion in accordance with an asset's contribution or functionality to a particular project, initiative, business unit, transaction, or a company as a whole.

A perhaps crude, but relevant, characterization of an asset's life cycle is akin to what a doctor once told me about the need for a particular prescription medicine: you will know when you don't need it anymore when you start forgetting to take it and realize you're feeling fine without it.

The cyclic aspect to intangible assets' value renders most conventional asset valuation techniques less relevant and certainly less useful, because they do not factor in threats to assets that can literally diminish their contributory value to nothing almost instantaneously, and provide little, if any, strategic post-transaction context to certain intangible assets' contributory value, in light of the consistent presence of asset risks and threats.

At the point in time in which an asset no longer carries the value it once did, there is less need to devote time and costly resources to preserving its proprietary status and value. Those resources and that time should be devoted elsewhere, perhaps to newly developed and more valuable intangible assets.

Safeguarding Intangible Assets

A prudent requisite to proposing any new business initiative is that it be accompanied by a compelling business case. The term *business case* should be normative in both content and context by incorporating projections of:

- Return-on-investment
- Margins

- Marketing
- Pricing
- Sustainability

With respect to the still relatively new practice of safeguarding intangible assets, a key starting point for management teams is recognition of their economic potential.

In this regard, a compelling business case for safeguarding intangible assets should, at minimum, include the following:

1. Demonstrate ways to quantify return-on-investment, by effectively articulating intangible asset safeguard (IAS) services to decision makers in ways that build credibility with intangible asset practitioners.
2. Demonstrate precisely what benefits a company can expect to receive by describing how and when stages of net present value (NPV) will be realized for the organization.
3. Demonstrate how the business case should fill an existing procedural void, strengthen an existing process, and it's not merely a duplication or new twist to an existing service or procedure.
4. Incorporate an organization's culture and operating characteristics in terms of key factors of decision makers' receptivity to new initiatives.
5. Demonstrate how IAS specialists can bring forward-looking clarity to conventional perspectives of business risk-taking by preventing losses or depreciation of intangible assets' contributory value.
6. Demonstrate that intangible assets and competitive advantages should no longer be accepted as just another risk of doing business, which organizations may knowingly or inadvertently assume as preludes to developing new markets or products.
7. Know precisely, in return-on-security-investment terms *what* must be measured, *how* it is to be measured, *when it* can be measured. See Chapter 3 on due diligence.
8. Avoid portraying IAS services as merely a snapshot-in-time process. IAS specialists' perspective should be flexible and self-adjusting as circumstances warrant—that is, as asset value risk cycles change or fluctuate.
9. Draw attention to the professional responsibilities of intangible asset strategists: they will facilitate and enable more secure, sustainable, and lucrative transactions; and they will increase the probability that when a deal or exit strategy is being planned and executed the value of an organization's intangible assets, proprietary competitive advantages, and IP will remain stable and intact.

Prosecuting Intangible Asset Losses

This section represents an issue every CSO, CIPO, CISO, CTO, CRO, and corporate legal counsel should, if they haven't already, fully consider. Having taught in a university criminology department for 20 years, it's less than rocket science to know that theft has conventionally been taught as involving some manner of misappropriation of things—that is, tangible, physical property.

However, an intriguing question was posed by Stuart Green (2012), a Rutgers University law professor. He asks whether the terms *theft* and *stealing* fit today's circumstances, particularly when the assets stolen or misappropriated are likely to be nonphysical in nature.

For most prosecutors, and obviously the music and movie industries to name a couple, it's easy to assume they prefer the relevant institutions continue to apply the terms *theft*, *stealing*, and *misappropriation* using conventional and time-honored language that essentially does not distinguish tangible from intangible assets. However, in the current knowledge-based global transaction economy, it does beg the legal question: Are those conventional, time-honored definitions about theft relevant to intangible assets?

To add complexity, but, perhaps reality, to this position, is that when particular types of intangible assets are stolen, the rightful owner is likely to retain some or perhaps even complete use of those assets, albeit perhaps in a depreciated or undermined form, because had they remained intact, they presumably could have delivered additional sources of revenue.

The reality is, companies are producing, acquiring, and inventing significantly fewer tangible things in lieu of assets that are more likely to be nonphysical. So, how does this very real circumstance mesh with the conventional perspective of property theft and stealing? Various courts and legislative bodies have periodically adjusted some of the conventional theft laws, according to Green (2012). However, has the time come for specialized legal doctrines to be developed to specifically reflect the theft of intangible assets?

In the mid-1960s, some criminal law reformers became frustrated with how courts and legal practitioners were distinguishing tangible and intangible property. One outcome of this frustration was that the American Law Institute developed a model penal code that essentially defined property as constituting *anything of value*. I remain unconvinced this was the most appropriate way to handle this. Admittedly, however, in 1962, intangible assets were hardly in mainstream business or legal vocabulary. Presumably then, when intangible assets succumb to theft or misappropriation, they should be treated uniformly.

Today, of course, intangible asset-driven businesses have sprouted globally, brimming full of intellectual, relationship, and structural capital, patents, brand, reputation, and often copyrighted material, each of which play increasingly important economic and competitive-advantage roles in profitability, sustainability, and growth potential. There is, of course, a range of empirical studies that reveal that a significant moral distinction exists between illegal file sharing and theft of physical property, even when the value of the properties is approximately the same.

Illegal downloading is, of course, a real and persistent problem that in all likelihood will not be going away anytime soon. Individuals work hard to produce creative works and are entitled to enjoy legal protection as well as reaping any economic benefits from their efforts. If others want to enjoy those creative works, it's reasonable to make them pay for the privilege.

Continuing to frame illegal downloading as a form of stealing probably warrants some review by companies. Companies may better position themselves if they consider a range of legal concepts that fit the nature and elements of the problem more appropriately—the first being to fully understand intangible assets. The most effective fix does not lie solely in terminology!

Information Security and Information Asset Protection

If a "hole" is found in a company's or its client's proprietary information "fence," the job of information security is to patch the hole; but, the job of an information asset protection specialist is, in addition to helping patch the hole, to determine:

- What caused the hole in the fence to occur in the first place, and were there precipitating circumstance or triggering factors?
- Under what circumstances was the hole in the fence initially discovered?
- Who, if anyone, knew the hole in the fence existed before it was discovered, but did not report it?
- How long did the hole in the fence exist before it was discovered?
- What information assets moved through the hole in the fence before it was discovered and patched?
- Is there evidence that the information-based assets that moved through the hole in the fence before it was discovered and patched were specifically targeted or merely arbitrarily acquired?
- How much economic hemorrhaging or impairment to asset value, materiality, competitive advantage, brand, reputation, ownership, trade secrecy, and strategic planning occurred as a result of information assets moving through the hole in the fence?
- Is it known who the recipients of the information assets that moved through the hole in the fence are, before it was discovered and patched?
- How will the recipients likely use or exploit those information assets?

The responsibilities of information asset protection specialists are now cross-functional and converge with risk management, human resources, IT security, intellectual property counsel, audits, valuation, R&D, reputation risk, and brand integrity, among others.

To mitigate adverse effects of information asset losses, an important key is to collaborate with information security with a singular objective: to preserve control, use, and ownership, and monitor the value and materiality of a company's information-based assets (Brenner).

New Product Launches and Due Diligence

Achieving successful and sustainable new product and innovation launches is increasingly dependent on management teams recognizing the following:

■ More than 80% of an innovation's value, projected sources of revenue, and potential building blocks for growth and expansion evolve directly from the contributory nature and value of intangible assets.
■ The importance that must be attached to ensuring the "innovation genie" remains in its respective bottle through its respective life cycle—that is, effectively protecting control, use, ownership, and defensibility of the innovation's key elements.

Continuous monitoring of key aspects of the innovation's status is critical. A key reason is that the absence of effective innovation asset management and oversight can and frequently does lead to misappropriation, theft, product counterfeiting, or piracy. If any one of those threats materializes, it would undermine product launch success and adversely affect the innovation's value, competitive advantages, and relevance within its market space.

An essential requisite for any innovation management team who aspires to achieve even partial recovery of their compromised innovation is having effective monitoring practices in place to not just prevent or mitigate any adverse effects from materialized risks, but also to know precisely when a compromise occurred and the precipitating factors. See Chapter 3 for information on conducting a thorough intangible asset competitive advantage assessment, which should be done immediately following a compromise to determine precisely what aspects of the innovation were actually compromised and how it will impact the product's launch and the business as a whole. This assessment and business impact analysis are, of course, essential to achieving any semblance of hope of recovering any of the innovation's assets.

Realistically, returning an innovation to its rightful owners, in a manner in which some or, more preferably, most of its market space competitive advantages remain reasonably intact, is not particularly successful in today's increasingly predatorial business environment.

There are many different views about what it takes to sustain a successful new product or idea launch and its eventual commercialization. Obviously, having a very attractive and commercializable product along with sufficient capital to execute a well-researched business plan and marketing strategy represent a couple of the traditional and necessary ingredients. It is the responsibility of the management team to unravel how those assets individually and collectively contribute to an innovation and then convert that into value.

Systemic Risks: Intellectual Property and Intangible Assets

The term *systemic risk* has a relatively long history. Its revival, in terms of becoming the business and legislative explanation for the calamities affecting the financial services sector beginning in the fall of 2008, has now come to be embedded in business lexicon to represent a broad cross-section of risk to various categories of assets, including intangible ones.

One of the better definitions of systemic risk, in my view, is provided by Steven Schwarcz (2008), of Duke University School of Law: "the probability that cumulative losses will occur from an event that ignites a series of successive losses along a chain of (financial) institutions or markets comprising a system."

Commonly embedded throughout the various definitions of systemic risk is the concept of a "triggering event." This is something that causes an internal or external cascading of adverse consequences. In the case of companies with fairly intensive portfolios of intellectual property and other forms of intangible assets, a triggering event could include theft, misappropriation, infringement, or premature leakage of key intangible assets, such as plans, intentions, or capabilities, or significant counterfeiting or product piracy operations against company-produced intangible assets.

Should any one of these adverse events occur, it would, with little doubt, collectively undermine or stifle asset value, competitive position, sources of revenue, and future growth opportunities. As far as intangible assets are concerned, systemic risks would also represent those assets cumulative risk. That is, loss or compromise of any intangible assets can rapidly and adversely ripple throughout a company and its entire chain of stakeholders.

Several studies report that systemic risks to a company's intellectual property and other forms of intangible assets lies largely with insiders with the proliferation of sophisticated and predatorial data mining, information brokering, infringement, misappropriation, and counterfeiting operations that function profitably on a global scale. Guesstimations of value losses for U.S. companies range from $45 to $200 billion annually (Trends in Proprietary Information Loss Survey, 2007; The Epoch Times, 2013).

References

Brenner, J., 2011. American the vulnerable: inside the new threat matrix of digital espionage, crime, and warfare. Penguin Press, New York.

Green, S., 2012. When stealing isn't stealing. New York Times Opinion.

Steven L., Schwarcz, 2008. Systemic risk. Georgetown Law J. 97, 193–249.

Trends in Proprietary Information Loss Survey, 2007. American Society for Industrial Security International and the National Counterintelligence Executive and ASIS Foundation.

The Epoch Times, 2013. The staggering cost of Economic Espionage against the U.S. Remarks by General Keith Alexander, Director, National Security Agency.

Company Culture

Investing in Company Culture Building

David Lapin (2012a) projects the next big wave of growth in business will come from businesses of which leaders and management team members know how to convert the intangible asset of a company's culture into high bottom-line value. Investing in building and nurturing a company's culture is the wisest investment any business leader or management team can make! Financially, it is a low-cost investment with a high probability of economic returns.

A company's culture is somewhat akin to a garden—that is, a culture will develop whether or not business leaders or management teams put forth the time and effort to actually design it. So, like a garden, if a company's culture is ignored or neglected—that is, absent regular management, oversight, and nurturing—it's very likely it will continue to grow regardless, but probably not as intended or preferred, and in ways that are not particularly helpful to the company and its mission. Adverse examples of this include inhibiting innovation or manifesting employee under-performance. Company cultures that evolve in this manner are said to be akin to an "invisible force" that cannot only undermine productivity but sap team leaders' energy.

Cultivating A Positive Company Culture

Developing, cultivating, and sustaining a desired company culture requires thought, wisdom, time, and some intellectual curiosity and emotional investment to understand what motivates employees to perform consistently well, even beyond expectations. There is no specific, one-size-fits-all methodology or strategy to achieve this, but there is ample anecdotal evidence and examples that good team leaders pay attention to it.

As Lapin (2012a) points out in his research, an authentic company culture is something competitors will find challenging if not impossible to imitate. Company culture is an intangible asset that, in most instances, can be commoditized and converted to real value. The knowledge-based global economy has allowed many leaders and managers to acquire a better understanding and appreciation for homegrown intangible assets like intellectual, structural, and relationship capital, and their potential for conversion as specialized commodities into value, revenue, reputation, and goodwill.

Many would agree with the view that Southwest Airlines (SWA, headquartered in Phoenix, AZ) is a prime example of a leader's ability to not only create a very open and transparent company culture, but also turn the intangible assets emanating from that culture into commodities with substantial monetary value. SWA has long been a dominant player with U.S. airline deregulation, and now in the ever-merging U.S.-based airline industry. Their growth is in part due to their operating culture being built upon genuine efficiencies—for example, flying only one model of aircraft, creating a no-frill travel experience, and no food service or preassigned seating. Ultimately, SWA has stripped most of the tangible commodities associated with conventional airline travel. In return, SWA's customers receive something of relatively equal value in return, at least in the eyes of their growing number of customers: a good flying experience underwritten by a culture embedded with intangible assets, such as joke-telling entertainment from flight attendants coupled with a felt sense of care.

There are three well-known "secrets" that underlie SWA's travel experience and its overall financial success since its inception:

1. The company and its leader, Herb Kelleher, built a culture that incorporates fun, entertainment, and care.
2. The culture feels authentic and genuine by passengers.
3. SWA has been able to convert its now intangible asset-based company culture into tangible benefits, including market share growth.

Numerous business schools today use SWA and its founder Herb Kelleher as a case study of commoditizing a company culture and its intangible competitive advantages balanced with tangible operational efficiencies.

While SWA was investing in and building its intangible asset-based company culture, numerous competitors were cutting financial corners that frequently eroded their own culture. Kelleher and SWA, on the other hand, only cut those financial corners that they presumably believed would have little or no impact on the culture they were building and passengers' overall travel experience. In fact, SWA continued to invest more in its culture even during periods when the airline industry, as a whole, was struggling. Kelleher and SWA management teams obviously recognize safe and on-time flights for passengers are, in essence, common commodities that competitors also provide to their passengers.

So, for SWA to be competitive in a deregulated environment, Kelleher and his management team purposefully built a company culture that would offer intangible assets that competitors couldn't or wouldn't. These assets have become well-publicized differentiators that are embedded in the company's values rather than directly in its products, processes, or structures. Products, processes, and structure can and will be copied, but intangible assets such as an authentic company culture cannot be readily copied, providing it is genuinely embedded in company and employee values.

Any company can build its own culture, one that is unique and innate to its people and strategic objectives. But when a company tries to copy another company's culture they quickly find it difficult, if not impossible, to replicate. Numerous SWA competitors have tried, over the years, to imitate SWA, but most fell short because they were unable, for whatever reason, to embed it in their company's values.

Creating A Company Culture: A Necessity, Not A Luxury

Imagine a person from another planet turning up at a funeral here on Earth. Without having to be told, he would know that a funeral is not an appropriate place to tell jokes. According to David Lapin (2012b) in his article 'How Intangible Corporate Culture Creates Tangible Profits,' scholars such as Harvard Professor Michael Tushman suggests this is the meaning of culture.

But culture does more than inform employees what attitudes and behaviors are expected of them. Culture reflects a company's soul and is responsible for generating human energy. This section is written with the intent that it respectfully encourages business leaders and management teams to recognize the importance of creating a company culture that converges with its intangible assets, particularly its intellectual, structural, and relationship capital.

EVERY COMPANY HAS A CULTURE

Whether by accident or by design, it is highly likely every company has a culture, says Dr. Philip E. Atkinson (2004). However, in most instances, Atkinson suggests, a company's culture is frequently a matter of accident or, simply, luck. Unfortunately, in numerous instances, Atkinson found, a company's culture may not match its strategy, its business plan, or its commercial intentions. In other words, a company culture may actually be counter to its needs. Further, Atkinson suggests, it's not unusual to observe a company culture that actually drives clients and customers away because its focus is primarily internal to the exclusion of being sufficiently customer- or client-oriented.

EXAMINE COMPANY CULTURE

A well-designed, configured, and balanced company culture that genuinely reflects each relevant component of a company's mission can be a very valuable intangible asset that delivers competitive advantages in multiples. It's prudent then for business leaders and management teams to assume an obligation, if not a fiduciary responsibility, to periodically examine and assess their company's culture for balance, match, and resilience.

There is ample evidence, along with just plain business sense, that for numerous companies globally, success—measured as elevated value, expanded sources of revenue, opportunities for growth, profitability, and sustainability—flows from an agreeable and well-executed company culture.

KEY COMPONENTS OF AN EFFECTIVE COMPANY CULTURE

The key components of this type of company culture are that it respectfully harnesses, exploits, and utilizes its intangible assets, such as intellectual, structural, and relationship capital. In most instances, these and other intangible assets are accepted, shared, and ultimately embedded in company practices and processes.

A RESILIENT COMPANY CULTURE

A company culture's resilience is indeed important, and a facet that should not be taken for granted or otherwise overlooked. A culture's resilience translates to how receptive and readily adaptive it is to the increasingly nuanced types of global, multipartnered, and multicultural business transactions that are common today.

A well-designed and executed company culture, recognized as a culmination of intangible assets, will deliver superior performance, providing, of course, resilience and sustainability have been prominently embedded along with a balanced internal/external orientation that reflects the company's mission and achieves competitive advantages relative to its respective industry sector.

However, company cultures require working in ambiguous and perhaps subjective arenas, relative to how company beliefs and values eventually surface as accepted processes, practices, group dynamics, and ultimately expected behaviors.

THIS CULTURE HAS TO CHANGE

Atkinson (2004) appropriately asks, how many times has the phrase "this culture has to change" been uttered by business leaders and management teams? To be sure, in recent years we have heard this phrase often relative to the global banking crisis, the recent exposures about the media, the publishing of Edward Snowden's revelations, the continued poor performance of educational systems, and the list goes on.

Respecting Atkinson's (2004) near-term as well as future research regarding company culture, it's certainly not challenging to infer a significant percentage of company cultures are not, or they are ineffectively, aligned with a company's mission, the various transactions it becomes engaged in, or its purpose. Surely, at some point, business leaders and management teams will recognize that it does not require publicly embarrassing revelations or investigations that produce substantial and long-lasting risk to a company's reputation to recognize that remedial company culture action is necessary and is the absolute correct thing to do.

It is a good idea to bring more clarity here about precisely what company culture actually is and how it can be built, shaped, installed, nurtured, monitored, and sustained.

REMEMBER: A COMPANY'S CULTURE IS AN INTANGIBLE ASSET

A company's culture should be or become *the* driving underlier to a company's forward movement, Atkinson (2004) suggests. More specifically, a company culture consists of its infrastructure and the proverbial glue that connect employees and processes (structural capital) to generate positive outcomes and results while being aligned with the business plan and vision for the future.

So, for 2014 and beyond, it's important that business leaders and management teams recognize, whether by accident, design, or luck, their company already has a functioning culture in place. The assessment that must be performed, however, is whether that culture meshes with the company's strategy, business plans, and overall commercial intentions. If not, often with slight modifications, managerial nurturing, and time, the existing culture can be reoriented to better connect with a company's needs.

Company Cultures: Their Future Must Accommodate Intangible Assets

I assume many readers are like me—that is, we only periodically give the notion of company culture much genuine thought. But, if asked, we could readily utter a sufficient number of adjectives, adverbs, and nouns that, once organized, would paint a fairly detailed operational portrait of our employer that would reveal the intricacies of our employer's company culture.

However, while we may understand how a company culture should be conveyed, many of us may not realize how important company culture has become in today's businesses as a valuable contributor to sources of revenue, competitive advantages, and overall sustainability—valuable intangible assets.

In their book *Rise of the DEO: Leadership by Design*, Maria Giudice and Christopher Ireland (2013) explain their view of the importance for companies to have a "design" executive officer in the place. Of the six defining characteristics that Giudice and Ireland believe DEOs should possess, a particularly relevant one is being a systems thinker, which they define as follows:

> *Despite their desire to disrupt and take risks, DEOs understand the interconnectedness of the work environment as a whole—that is, they recognize each part of the organization (probably) overlaps and influences other parts of the organization. They also recognize unseen connections that surround what's actually visible within a company which helps give their disruptions intended, rather than chaotic, impact and makes their risk taking more conscious.*

More specifically, Giudice and Ireland suggest that business leaders who actually understand the transformative power and influence of a company culture design and embrace and engage its characteristics will lead in times of change. Thus, recognizing the value intangible assets have for a company constitutes change, and leading that culture change is not merely important, it's a necessity.

Company Culture Due Diligence

A company initiating, or even contemplating, a merger or acquisition would be well served today if a company culture analysis was included in their overall due diligence strategy (see also Chapter 3 on due diligence). The reason, as conveyed here many times, is that more than 80% of most companies' value and sources of revenue either lie in or directly evolve from intangible assets, which company culture is one.

From an operational perspective, intellectual and structural capital constitutes the know-how and processes that collectively underlie the revenue, competitive advantages, and efficiencies being sought by a company. So, in merger and acquisition transactions, management teams are obliged to understand that intangible assets are indivisible from a company's culture that connects and bonds companies, employees, and stakeholders together.

Grant McCracken (2009), one of several prominent company culture specialists today, specializes in the intersection of commerce and culture—that is, where company culture sits at the intersection of anthropology and economics. From McCracken's and others' work in this arena, we see perspectives emerging, that company culture is being likened to an internal version of a company's brand. That is largely attributable to a broader recognition of the reality that company culture generally encompasses a company's mission, its vision, its values, and its intangible assets. Clearly, McCracken understands how an effective company culture can impact a business; he often emphasizes that a company's culture is marketing's newest version of the proverbial "silver bullet."

But, before embarking on a company culture analysis, says Monica Mehta (2009), a writer for *Profit* and *Profit Online*, the target company should be distinguished on several cultural dimensions, often conveyed as dimensions between two extremes. There should be less resistance to including company culture analysis as an integral component to transaction due diligence. It is important to realize, as Mehta points out, that there may be no necessarily right or wrong company culture at the analysis stage. The initial key is that due diligence teams are operationally familiar with the characteristics and features of their own company's culture.

Mehta uses two examples as a comparison. The following can be observed with respect to Company 1:

- It's engaged in public manufacturing with a strong western, primarily U.S.-oriented, business culture.
- The nodes confirm the company has an individualized work ethic orientation overall wherein employees have the opportunity to work in a meritocracy fashion.
- It's rules-oriented—that is, there is a process for most every function or task.
- It has a relatively short-term focus—for example, new business strategies need to produce a return-on-investment within each fiscal year.
- Managers assume employees are self-motivated to perform well providing their efforts are duly and appropriately recognized, such as through a bonus program.
- It's relatively internally focused, and plans its business using a traditional budget scheme.
- It benefits from the best practices of performance management—that is, a top-down strategy for task implementation, coupled with openly shared feedback with a ranking of the best-scoring people in sales.

Company 2 would likely not be as successful because:

- It has been a family-owned business for multiple generations with senior management knowing most of the employees, many of whom have worked for the company their entire professional lives.
- The next generation of ownership is growing up and the company needs to secure their future too.
- The culture of the company is externally focused, which suggests it can only survive in the market by sustaining its extreme customer focus.
- Of the company's decision-making process, senior management ask for input only from a few trusted employees, and then the family makes a decision with information eventually being shared with the staff, but usually verbally and in informal meetings.
- While the company has performance indicators, they are mostly aimed at how the company is performing in the eyes of the customers.
- Rewards are not directly tied to performance during a specific period; rather the family rewards loyalty and provides bonuses when deemed necessary.

If Company 2 is realizing losses, perhaps some elements of the performance management practices of Company 1 need to be adopted. Conversely, if Company 1 is experiencing a substantial growth phase, key people (and their respective intellectual, structural, and relationship capital abilities) need to be retained to manage that growth with these individuals becoming part of the company's inner circle of strategic thinkers and decision makers.

Thus, the insight that a company culture analysis (due diligence) would bring to transaction oversight could ultimately set a strategic path how performance management should be conceived and implemented. But, transaction management teams should also recognize that performance management can work as a measurement mechanism that drives employee behavior.

So, if there are particular aspects of a target company's culture that appear undesirable or otherwise may impede a transaction's projected milestones for success, they may warrant change. Otherwise, if there is too much of a group focus, individual performance indicators may be useful; of a long-term focus, short-term targets may help; or if relationship focus turns into nepotism, more uniform reward processes may be needed.

Company Reputation and Financial Performance

As noted earlier in this chapter, a company's reputation is an intangible asset. More company management teams should devote time assessing various strategies to leverage their reputation to create competitive advantages that will distinguish their company from others that operate in the same sector.

First, a broadly agreed-on definition of *company culture* is warranted here. Chatman and Cha (2003) describe it as "a system of shared values which define what is important and norms that define appropriate attitudes and behavior" (p. 21). Thus, it's easy to surmise that a strong and well-managed company culture can actually influence a company's financial performance, because the shared and strongly held norms and values embedded in the company culture serve to increase behavioral consistency among employees. This, in turn, can lead to enhanced coordination and control, improved goal alignment, and increased employee effort (Sorenson, 2002, p. 70–72).

Relatively few researchers have empirically tested the relationship between company culture and reputation as Flatt and Kowalczyk (2006) have. They demonstrated this relationship by engaging 104 companies (as part of their research project) in which, among other things, they found that company culture not only enhances financial performance, but also is positively related to reputation itself; thus, reputation functions somewhat as a mediator between culture and financial performance. Flatt and Kowalczyk's paper extends prior research in this arena by examining the direct and indirect effects of culture and reputation on financial performance, and tests if reputation actually mediates the effect of culture on financial performance. Flatt and Kowalczyk admit, however, while there is fairly broad support that financial performance is a predictor of reputation, less is known about what other variables may also be predictors of a strong, positive, and possibly resilient reputation.

Fombrun (1996) states that "a company's reputation sits on the bedrock of its identity, i.e., the core values that shape it's … communications, culture, and decisions" (p. 268). Further, a company's identity, in turn, is closely aligned with its … character, personality, and culture" (p. 277). Therefore, core cultural values, such as credibility, reliability, trustworthiness, and responsibility are at the core of the perceptual representation of a company's reputation (Fombrun, 1996). Thus, company culture provides the context for how a company's identity is formed and articulated in relation to its cultural context (Hatch and Schultz, 2000, p. 25).

The continued quest to identify various and key variables that are consistent predictors of a company's reputation is essential, because without this insight, neither academic researchers nor company leadership and management teams will be able to advise companies about strategies to enhance their reputation to achieve competitive advantage and increase their financial performance.

Performance-Based Company Culture

In 1987, the former and now late Nucor Steel CEO F. Kenneth Iverson embarked on an admittedly risky proposition (business model) at the time, in which he came to embrace the perspective that most employees (at Nucor) would likely perform better if they were provided with what were deemed quite innovative incentives (Byrnes and Arndt, 2006).

Iverson himself was the driving force for developing a uniquely egalitarian (companywide) culture for Nucor. The key differentiator for this particular company culture sprung from its employee performance-based features. Iverson set in motion a culture to empower Nucor's employees with probably the most significant tool in any management teams' toolbox at that time: to treat the employees with respect. As such, an integral component embedded in Nucor's overall employee compensation strategy was designed to foster motivation and productivity on a companywide basis. That is, the salary reconstruction aspects of Nucor's company culture allowed for 66% of Nucor employees' weekly pay to be linked to performance, with up to 20% of this total coming from Nucor's profit-sharing program, which took 10% of operating profits and divided them among all employees (excluding senior officers).

Very simply, Iverson's premise was that by rewarding individual and collective employee productivity, rather than the conventional job title or higher-level degree methodologies, Nucor would be positioned to empower its employees to consistently work hard because risks and rewards were being shared, and would ultimately come to benefit stakeholders as well. Thus, individual employee empowerment, as a method for rewarding employee productivity, would ultimately fall to how well employees recognized and utilized their intellectual, structural, and relationship capital, each of which are intangible assets.

Therefore, the well-being of Nucor executives was dependent on the productivity of Nucor's employees. So, if productivity declined, employee salaries declined as well, but the CEO's salary and benefits declined also. Thus, employees knew that the same factors impacting their income also impacted executives, providing for a shared sense of risks and rewards on an enterprise-wide basis (Byrnes and Arndt, 2006).

However, a relevant question is: What is the absolute best and most objective method for capturing this contributory value when Nucor is sold? (http://en.wikipedia.org/wiki/Nucor)

A High-Performance Company Culture Is A Valuable Intangible Asset

Congratulations to management teams globally who recognize the importance of achieving a high-performing company culture. It's a worthy and generally lucrative strategic goal and a valuable intangible asset, which in today's increasingly competitive global business development and transaction environment is integral.

Of course, merely achieving a high-performing company culture is insufficient standing alone. It must be sustainable and strategic in orientation. That is, the culture itself requires consistent monitoring, nurturing, and assessment, and must be sufficiently adaptive to accommodate business development and transaction circumstances companies encounter globally.

Actually achieving a high-performance company culture, however, is dependent on factors such as a company's industry sector; the types of transactions a company typically engages in (i.e., what works, what does not work); the operating philosophy a company's employees and stakeholders have grown accustomed to (i.e., how things get done, how decisions get made); a company's receptivity to and operational familiarity with intangible assets in terms of how it recognizes (i.e., what gets rewarded, how and when), develops, and utilizes its intellectual, structural, and relationship capital.

While these and other factors will influence the outcome, a key to building a high-performance company culture is ensuring management teams have clearly defined where their company is headed strategically. This starts by identifying specific destination points, a timeframe that it needs to arrive at those destination points, what resources are required, and how those resources will be utilized to arrive at the destination points within the timeframe. The specifics of a high-performing culture are generally nuanced to every company—that is, there is no one-size-fits-all solution when it comes to culture building.

Torben Rick (2011), an internationally recognized management specialist, poses a salient question in one of his blog posts: Is company culture driving the strategy, or is it undermining it, or is culture more important than strategy? In support of his analysis, Rick identifies 11 key elements in creating a high-performance culture that he suggests will probably "fit" for most companies:

1. *Clearly define what winning looks like.* This can be achieved by looking across the entire company, then defining what it looks like from various functional perspectives, such as sales, marketing, customer service, procurement, and finance.
2. *Spell out the "preferred culture."* In much the same way that company leaders shape and communicate their company's vision, a preferred culture may consist of a set of guiding principles or sought-after values. However, the best, Rick suggests, go further by establishing "preferred behaviors" that support the preferred culture. This occurs by identifying and assessing particular aspects of a company's current culture that leaders are satisfied with, while also asking:
   - Which additional preferred behaviors does the company need to create for their preferred culture?
   - What behaviors are actually being rewarded and which unacceptable behaviors are merely being tolerated?
   - How does the company measure each of their preferred behaviors?
3. *Set stretch targets.* In most instances, employees rise to the standard being set for them. The more a company and its management team expects, in most

instances the more they will likely achieve. But there is a fine line between good stretch targets and bad ones. The good ones can energize a company, while the bad ones can dampen morale on an enterprise-wide basis.

4. *Connect to the big picture.* The majority of employees want to be a part of a compelling future and want to know what is most important at work and what excellence actually looks like. For targets to be meaningful and effective in motivating employees, the employees must be connected to a company's larger strategic goals. Employees who don't understand the role they play in company successes are more likely to become disengaged. No matter what level an employee is at, he or she should be able to articulate, with precision, how their efforts feed into their company's broader strategy.

5. *Develop an ownership mentality.* When employees understand the boundaries in which they can operate and maneuver, as well as where the company wants them to go, they will feel empowered with a freedom to decide and act, and most often make the right choices.

6. *Improve performance through transparency.* By sharing financial numbers with employees, a company can improve its performance. However, a company also needs to be sure their employees are trained to understand financial statements and have sufficient insight into their own jobs to know how to favorably affect the numbers. But, focus on additional metrics besides merely the financial ones.[1] This will allow employees to be better able to relate to the results and they will feel more included in the process as a whole.

7. *Increase performance through employee engagement.* Employees who are engaged in their positions and understand the contributory role and value to their employer are inclined to put more effort into their job and have the willingness to give more than is minimally required, hence a greater sense of personal committment and loyalty to the company.

8. *Storytelling is important.* Storytelling can be a powerful tool when a company wants to drive performance improvement. Leaders must be able use stories to motivate their employees to achieve more than they thought possible.

---

[1] For example, we were once teaching a financial-fundamentals class to managers of a division of a Fortune 100 company. Since we like to use real data, we asked the company to share with us the division's current revenue, costs, and other figures for classroom use. The company politely declined, saying it didn't want the managers to see the divisional statements, even though those very same numbers would soon appear publicly in the company's annual 10-K report. Talk about shooting yourself in the foot. And yet this company is hardly alone in its myopia. Our experience is that many, if not most companies, refuse to share much financial data with any employee other than top executives. The unfortunate message this sends to anyone outside the loop: We'll tell you what you need to know. Period (Berman and Knight, 2012).

9. *Communicate internally.* Internal communication is an important element of any change-management process like creating a company culture and therefore must be consistently engaged in the overall agenda. These five questions should be asked in regards to employees:

- Have they heard the message?
- Do they believe it?
- Do they know what it means?
- Have they interpreted it for themselves?
- Have they internalized it?

10. *Take the time to celebrate.* Taking the time to celebrate is important, because it acknowledges employees' hard work, boosts their morale, and helps sustain momentum—in other words, if you want something to grow, pour champagne on it!

11. *Don't take high-performing company cultures for granted.* High-performance organizations do not take their culture for granted. They plan it, monitor it, and manage it so that it remains aligned with what they want to achieve. All is for nothing if company management teams do not align the core mission of their company with its culture. After all, culture eats strategy for breakfast!

In 1964 in the pornography case *Jacobellis v. Ohio*, U.S. Supreme Court Justice Potter Stewart uttered a now-famous nonrational perspective: "I shall not today attempt further to define the kinds of material I understand to be embraced within that shorthand description; and perhaps I could never succeed in intelligibly doing so, but, I know it when I see it and the motion picture involved in this case is not that." In many respects, Justice Potter's perspective is quite similar to the way that company culture is often characterized—as somewhat of an invisible (intangible) temperament or attitude that links companies, employees, and stakeholders together.

References

Atkinson, P.E., 2004. Creating and shaping a performance-driven culture. Control 7, 21–26. <http://www.iomnet.org.uk/JournalResources/Journal.aspx>.

Berman, K., Knight, J., 2012. What your employees don't know will hurt you. Wall Street J. Rep. Leadership, 1.

Byrnes, N., Arndt, M., 2006. The art of motivation; what you can learn from a company that treats workers like owners. Inside the surprising performance culture of steelmaker Nucor. Business Week.

Chatman, J.A., Cha, S.E., 2003. Leading by Leveraging Culture. In: Chowdhury, S. (Ed.), Next Generation Business Series: Leadership Financial Times Prentice-Hall, Englewood Cliffs, NJ.

Flatt, S.J., Kowalczyk, S.J., 2006. Corporate Reputation as a Mediating Variable between Corporate Culture and Financial Performance, paper presented at the 2006 Reputation Institute Conference, New York. May 25–28.

Fombrun, C., 1996. Reputation: realizing value from the corporate linage. Harvard Business School Press, Boston, MA.

Giudice, M., Ireland, C., 2013. Rise of the DEO: Leadership by Design. New Riders, Upper Saddle River, NJ.

Jacobellis v. Ohio, 378 U.S. 184 (1964).

Lapin, D., 2012a. Lead by Greatness: Character Can Power Your Success. Avoda Books. Retrieved from<http://leadbygreatness.com>.

Lapin, D., 2012b. How Intangible Corporate Culture Creates Tangible Profits. <http://www.fastcompany.com/1840650/how-intangible-corporate-culture-creates-tangible-profits> (accessed 4 May 2014).

McCracken, G., 2009. Chief Culture Officer: How to Create a Living, Breathing Corporation. Basic Books, New York.

Mehta, M., 2009. Analyzing cultural performance management. <http://www.oracle.com/us/corporate/profit/features/122408-cultural-143806.html> (accessed 6 May 2014).

Rick, T., 2011. Top ten + key elements in creating a high performance culture. Meliorate (Torben Rick' blog).

Schultz, M., Hatch, M., 2000. The expressive organization: linking identity, reputation, and the corporate brand. Oxford University Press.

Sorenson, J.B., 2002, March. The strength of corporate culture and the reliability of firm performance. Adm. Sci. Q. 47, 70–91.

Chapter 6

Reputation Risks and Their Management

This chapter considers the persistent, increasingly adverse, and rapid effects of materialized reputation risks to companies globally. It's essential for management teams to recognize how universal and asymmetric reputation risks are today, and increasingly so for the foreseeable future; that virtually no company, irrespective of size, sector, or maturity, can expect to be immune to or free from reputation risks; and how reputation risk can, and usually does, cascade throughout an enterprise and to its various stakeholders.

Categories of Reputation Risk

Every company's reputation is an intangible asset. I have colleagues who regularly make a strong case that reputation risks are a distinctive and, therefore, a standalone risk category. That is, they are a type of risk that "cuts across" functional business units and other conventional boundaries. This is based, in large part, to the overlap and interconnectivity of the following seven categories of reputation risks (Bonime-Blanc, 2013):

1. Political risk
2. Operational risk
3. Financial risk
4. Technological risk
5. Legal risk
6. Supply-chain risk
7. Leadership and organizational culture risk

Every operating company globally is vulnerable to each of these seven risk categories. That said, each of the categories possesses distinctive aspects. Among the most prominent, perhaps, is that they evolve from different places or locations.

Each of these seven reputation risks should be prominently factored into any risk identification, management, and mitigation equation. That is, reputation risks are not always defined from separately or individually occurring events; rather, they can materialize singularly, collectively, or simultaneously, and rapidly cascade throughout an enterprise with adverse effects. Reputation risks can materialize in conjunction with any of the seven categories of risk. If the risk persists, but is not recognized or addressed, in all likelihood it will periodically reemerge over time.

Dr. Bonime-Blanc (2013) cites examples of each risk category in the context of reputation risk:

- *Political risk*: This type of risk will materialize based on geographic location. For instance: where there is instability of a country's political system and it's socio-political affairs; where leadership turnover is unpredictable and often violent; where civil liberties and due process go unprotected; where the division of government branches is ineffective with little or no judicial independence; and where regulatory oversight is politically influenced or exists with conflict of interests.
- *Operational risk*: This type of risk is frequently embedded in a company's operations, workforce, overall administration and organization, as well as its supply-chain and procurement programs. For example, it can emerge from ignoring local licensing or operating permit requirements; from business continuity, distribution, sales, and other business development channels; and from joint ventures, partnerships, and the management of local operations.
- *Financial risk*: This type of risk comes from improperly reporting or mischaracterizing earnings or expenses on financial statements or balance sheets. This can also include a company's financial and contractual interrelationships; the absence of internal controls; little or no oversight or attention paid to taxation, sales, business development, and financial incentives; as well as how the financial details of transactions are collected, reported, and disclosed throughout a company's or country's financial reporting chain.

- *Technological risk*: This type of risk comes from improper or inadequate safeguarding of intellectual property and proprietary information and data in ways that conflict with increasingly country-/resource-centric intellectual property laws. Technology risk also includes how well and the speed with which companies adapt to today's persistent and sophisticated cyber threats and vulnerabilities.
- *Legal risk*: This type of risk is caused from permitting or overlooking the subversion of a government-sanctioned law or regulatory compliance requirements, such as corruption, fraud, data privacy abuse, discrimination, harassment, antitrust violations, and money laundering.
- *Supply-chain risk*: This type of risk embodies multifaceted sets of risks starting at the supply chains' inception to the end of the supply chain. This includes supply-chain disruption; quality and integrity of ingredients; proper vetting of third-party providers; health, safety, and environmental compliance by factories; labor issues; and compliance and procurement planning to sustain supply-chain integrity and resilience. Supply-chain risk also includes overlooking or disregarding child labor in developing countries where a company's goods are being produced.
- *Leadership and organizational culture risk*: This type of risk results from allowing or encouraging a company culture to persist in which retribution, fear, or intimidation are routinely practiced—that is, an unscrupulous and corrupt company culture may be dismissive of regulatory compliance and risk management issues.

Reputation Risks Are A Separate Category of Risk

Each of the preceding risk types can be a distinct category of risk; therefore, when the risk materializes, it will become embedded in a company and will manifest as a top layer to more endemic reputation risk. Consequently, Dr. Bonime-Blanc (2013) suggests, ethical and effective leadership, coupled with an enterprise-wide culture of integrity, while challenging to measure and time consuming to develop and sustain, may truly be the absolute best form of reputation risk management.

An effective enterprise-wide reputation risk management initiative that recognizes the broad risk categories just described integrated with a root-cause analysis to ascertain where such risks may actually emerge, will help companies to identify and distinguish their salient reputation risks, assess reputation risk probabilities and criticalities, and contribute to a more realistic prioritization of reputation risks to achieve more effective decision-making and action planning.

However, reputation risk management action plans will be less effective if they do not demonstrate the linkage of the material risks back to a company's business plan and strategy as a whole. When that occurs, a company will realize strong multiplier effects. Of course, operational familiarity with reputation risks and commitment to preventing and mitigating them play key roles to any plan's success.

Employment Contractual Safeguards Can Mitigate Reputation Risk

Forward-looking companies, whether they be a university-based research spinoff, a start-up, an SMM (small or medium multinational), or a global Fortune 1000, is likely experiencing an increasingly competitive business transaction environment in regard to securing human and intellectual capital to sustain their competitive position, realize growth strategies, and achieve financial security.

Prospective candidates for employment can be readily identified from virtual pools of global applicants. However, a percentage of the candidates with the levels of experience, know-how, and trusted academic credentials are frequently already wrapped in various forms of noncompetes (NCs), nondisclosure agreements (NDAs), and other forms of confidentiality agreements (CAs) that have, quite wisely in most instances, become routine fixtures of employee hiring and on-boarding processes.

ESTABLISH BOUNDARIES

In most instances, the rationale underlying the requisite that employees enter into NCs, NDAs, or CAs is to establish boundaries that employees are legally and contractually obligated to work within, usually for a specified period of time, to safeguard their employer's proprietary information, trade secrets, and business processes.

These contracts create legal obligations to privacy that compel employee signatories to keep specified information secret and secured. Any form of contractual agreement that obligates employees to safeguard their employers' intellectual and structural capital related to work products, company proprietary information, and trade secrets will proactively inhibit a percentage of employees, from ever purposefully divulging specified information to individuals absent a right to know.

On the other hand, the reactive elements of CAs are executed primarily to establish legal standing or provide a recourse for a victimized company to seek criminal and/or civil charges against employee(s) who elect, for whatever reason, to at some point during their employment or post-employment period purposefully disregard the boundaries of a previously executed CA and divulge information to others.

SLOW ACCESS TO NEEDED INFORMATION

There is a perception, real or anecdotal, that CAs will limit or otherwise adversely affect the speed and collaborative necessities that come from sharing and disseminating information in a timely manner. Those actually responsible for information asset protection may not find this argument to be particularly credible.

Another relevant, but often overlooked, reality related to that is the contributory value of an employee's existing or future intellectual, structural, and relationship capital are indeed intangible assets, and exist as either standalone or in collaborative combinations. Therefore, companies may find proactive prudency in, at minimum, revisiting or rewriting then reexecuting an employee's CA, versus assuming its initial one-time execution is a sufficient inhibitor for the duration of an employee's employment.

For new hires—particularly, those who have been recruited for possessing specific intellectual and structural capital, presumably to advance a new or existing company initiative or project—should be subject to regular review. Seldom does an employee's intellectual and structural capital remain stationary relative to its contributory value. In most instances, such intangible (intellectual) assets will likely elevate and expand—that is, their contributory value will heighten—and, as such, become increasingly attractive commodities to economic adversaries globally.

AN INCOMING EMPLOYEE'S CA NEEDS TO BE THOROUGHLY UNRAVELED

An incoming employee's CA needs to be thoroughly unraveled, due, in part, to the duration, what is covered in an employee's former employer's CA, and whether there may be overlapping features. Thus, it's essential to unravel and assess these CAs for their relevance to the immediate impact on the hiring company, and the employee's ability to make immediate contributions. In other words, a company should be able to legally navigate such agreements to avoid, among other things, incurring extraordinarily embarrassing and costly reputation risks if an agreement is inadvertently or purposefully violated.

Also, in today's human resource (HR)-sensitive environment, any cultural, legal, and religious contexts embedded in a CA that could conceivably hamper or delay a new hire's eventual contributory value must be respectfully assessed.

There are instances in which new hires have either been purposefully or inadvertently remiss in fully understanding specifics contained in CAs executed with former employers. Some employees pay little or no attention to the language in CAs or perhaps don't fully comprehend the legal boundaries that their signed agreement actually imposes on them for the duration of their employment, not to mention periods of time following their employment with a new employer.

The time and attention devoted to unraveling and assessing prospective hires' previous employment CAs can help mitigate reputation risks, make for more informed hiring decisions, reduce the probability that potentially problematic employees will be inadvertently hired and create costly and long-term reputation risks. Being on the receiving end of an allegation of violating a CA can certainly undermine the contributory value of not only a new hire, but a company's overall reputation.

Unfortunately, the long-held adage "ignorance is bliss" in these circumstances is becoming more challenging to enforce in today's virtual and global recruitment and hiring environment. So, the onus is on every employer, throughout their respective new hire processes, to not just inquire, but bring absolute clarity to the boundaries of any and all employment CAs that may have an adverse effect on an employer's reputation should there be a breach.

Determinants of Reputation Risks

According to Robert Eccles and Scott Newquist, founders of Perception Partners, and Roland Schatz, founder of the Media Tenor Institute, there are three things that determine the extent to which a company is exposed to reputation risks (Eccles et al., 2007):

- Whether its reputation exceeds its true character.
- How much beliefs and expectations change externally, which can widen or (less likely) narrow the reputation reality gap.
- The quality of internal coordination, which also can affect the reputation reality gap.

Eccles and colleagues (2007) point out that effectively managing reputation risks must commence with recognizing that reputation is a matter of perception. Even disregarding the intuitive nature of this statement, one would be hard-pressed to find a more relevant truism for companies today. A company's overall reputation is a function of its reputation among its various stakeholders, which include investors, customers, suppliers, employees, regulators, politicians, and nongovernmental organizations; and the communities in which the firm operates and specific categories, such as product quality, corporate governance, employee relations, customer service, intellectual capital, financial performance, and handling of environmental and social issues.

A strong positive reputation among stakeholders across multiple categories will result in a strong positive reputation for the company overall.

Managing A Company's Reputation Risks Starts by Recognizing Reputation Is An Intangible Asset

Some suggest there is little need to distinguish company reputation risks because all risks can, and frequently do, adversely impact a company's reputation or standing among its customers, stakeholders, and investors. An increasingly exacerbating element to a company's reputation risks today is that it used to take years of poor management to destroy a company's reputation; today, a company's reputation can be seriously damaged if not destroyed almost overnight.

It's not just due to the expanded range and asymmetric nature of company exposures, vulnerabilities, and missteps that can so rapidly become public. It's also about the speed with which such risks cannot just strike, but rapidly cascade throughout an enterprise (internally and externally) and escalate to become a segment on the 24/7 global news cycles. This can produce costly consequences and long-lasting side effects, some of which, of course, become irreversible, or at minimum take months if not years for a company to return to a state of operational and financial normalcy.

An Opinion Research Corporation report states "reputation is as much about perception and the perception of behaviors, as it is about fact" (Resnick, 2006). Reputation, the ORC report states, is about expectations, ethics, trust, relationships, confidence, and integrity, each of which are built and sustained on the fundamental belief that management teams and boards possess and consistently practice those characteristics.

A reputation risk management plan then:

- Should recognize the asymmetric nature that most reputation risks assume today.
- Is best approached as a company-wide responsibility.
- Should be designed to recognize and distinguish particularly adverse reputation risks at their emerging stages that carry a potential for cascading quickly and early.
- Should include immediately available means (internal and external) to effectively assess and rapidly mount an initiative directed toward mitigating potential cascading affects.

Certainly within the past decade it was relatively common and sometimes even an advisable and prudent practice to measure a company's risk tolerance level. In other words, risks that would materialize within the risk tolerance levels would presumably permit a company to continue to operate within its range of normalcy. Today, however, for the reasons already conveyed, reputation risks that may initially be characterized as falling within preconceived levels of tolerance can escalate and cascade so rapidly that each reputation risk warrants rapid and objective assessment, not solely on the basis of a company's conventional risk tolerance levels or appetite, but based on the probability that the risks will evolve in a manner to actually affect reputation adversely.

Seldom Can Company Reputation be Manufactured

Seldom can a company's reputation be manufactured—that is, evolve from a single advertising campaign or public relations initiative. Rather, a company's reputation is built on consistently meeting and exceeding customer, client, stakeholder, and investor expectations, particularly those perceived as being consistent with the values being conveyed and claimed by the company, and any perceived promises the company makes through its stakeholder marketing and communication initiatives—that is, "walking the talk."

Only those management teams who are out-of-step or naïve with respect to the realities of today's 24/7 global business news cycles and instantaneous social media functionalities would characterize reputation risks as merely being temporary problems that can be preempted, mitigated, diffused, or quickly remediated through conventional public relations initiatives. Today, company reputation risk challenges can be observed unraveling in real time via cable news networks and social media and are very substantive "wake-up calls" for management teams to immediately and objectively examine how or whether their internal operating culture is genuinely reflective of its public behavior and the range of expectations of customers, consumers, clients, stakeholders, investors, and the global public at-large.

The demise in 2002 of Arthur Andersen Company is attributed to irreparable reputational damage following terrible publicity the company received related to the Enron scandal. More recently, BP incurred significant reputation damage relative to its association with the Deepwater Horizon explosion in the Gulf of Mexico in 2010 (Kendrick, 2013).

There are countless other examples, but a positive and resilient reputation helps companies to deal more effectively with future reputation risk events, should they occur, because it creates a reserve of goodwill that can help the business to better endure these events.

ACE's survey also notes that 4 out of 5 executives surveyed stated they regard their company's reputation as its most significant asset. Nothing particularly new here! But, despite evidence there is a growing understanding and appreciation for materialized reputation risks and their adverse impact on companies, one of the major challenges survey respondents revealed is quite straightforward: "getting their head around" the asymmetric and otherwise intangible nature of reputation risks. More specifically, 9 of 10 survey respondents reported that company reputation risks is "the most difficult risk category to manage."

Reputation risks are different from other risks. It is difficult to define, measure, and, therefore, manage—a task made more complicated by uncertainty over who "owns" the issue inside companies.

Also revealed from ACE's report are respondents' citing what they believe are factors that contribute to today's growing corporate reputation risk environment. ACE's survey respondents expressed particular concern about the following trends that are influencing and elevating reputation risk levels:

- Expanding global footprints and increasingly complex and risk-laden supply chains.
- Increasingly dynamic and challenging regulatory environments from which compliance is now considered to be a core competence in many industries. With failure to manage regulatory change effectively this will inevitably lead to serious reputational damage.
- Rapid company expansion into new markets and the challenges associated with maintaining consistent (ethical, business, product) practices and standards in a boundary-less transaction environment.

The survey's respondents reported that damage to customer relationships and the adverse financial impact of materialized reputation risks; the speed at which reputation risks can materialize and cascade throughout a company and its supply chain; and the reality that reputation risks can emerge from anywhere, at any time, and from any place within a company or along its stakeholder or supply chain make reputation risks more difficult to predict.

Interestingly, and quite revealing, is the fact that respondents to ACE's survey cited particular areas where companies judge themselves to be the weakest at reputation risk management:

- Measuring external perceptions of the company.
- Quantifying the financial impact of reputation risks, and because reputation risk impact is more difficult to quantify, it frequently makes it less well understood compared to tangible risks and threats.
- Restoring company reputation after reputation risk incidents have materialized.
- The absence of effective counsel about how to manage reputation risks, which elevates the sense of uncertainty and confusion about how best to manage reputation risks.

Fewer than one-third of companies believe they are well prepared to address these issues.

The Role of Company Chief Security Officers

While I am confident most chief security officers (CSOs) recognize the increasing relevance and importance of managing reputation risks on behalf of their employer, there is little, if any, substantive or objective data that describes the actual percentage of CSOs who now have been tasked with those specific responsibilities.

CSOs are well positioned to be the "first responders" to materializing reputation risks. Many existing CSO responsibilities are directly or indirectly related to safeguarding their employer's reputation. What is necessary now is to bring a stronger sense of business clarity to those responsibilities through current examples of reputation risks gone awry; by identifying the various dimensions to reputation risks that have materialized regionally, nationally, and internationally, and not merely those affecting the Fortune 500 companies; and the various ways materialized reputation risks can adversely impact a company economically, competitively, and strategically.

There is growing evidence that reputation risks that materialize are precipitated by some type of breach, compromise, or other adverse activity involving insiders—that is, a company's employees. CSOs then represent those most knowledgeable and generally best positioned in terms of familiarity with a company's internal and external environment, to recognize and proactively address reputation risks, particularly those initiated by insiders.

Reputation Risk-Intelligent Company Culture and Organizational Resilience

A good first step in developing a reputation risk-intelligent company culture is recognizing that risks are not solely an external phenomenon. An equally important step comes from recognizing that company value can be favorably affected by integrating risk management and human resource management. The rationale for doing so lies in the reality that a significant percentage of company risks actually evolve from employee actions, including management team and board members.

In terms of actually laying the foundation for developing a reputation risk-intelligent company culture, CSOs will find it prudent to recognize that it can be best executed at the point when the following converge:

- *Risk governance:* How a company treats risks and assumes responsibility for risk oversight and strategic decision making.
- *Risk infrastructure management:* How a company assumes responsibility for and understands how to design, implement, oversee, and sustain a risk management program.
- *Risk ownership:* Employees becoming operationally familiar with what their risk responsibilities are—that is, they assume some responsibility for identifying, measuring, monitoring, and reporting risks.

Becoming more intelligent and objective about a company's reputation risks are essential preludes to creating a risk-intelligent company culture wherein management teams assume a responsibility for elevating and cultivating a company-wide awareness and operational familiarity about the materialization of reputation risks. This begins by adopting common definitions of reputation risks in accordance with developing standards and best practices relative to a company's industry sector, operating locales, and converging law, and defining roles, responsibilities, and authority for managing reputation risks with necessary levels of transparency.

The focal points and deliverables of reputation risks are, as suggested previously, already woven into corporate security and risk management functions by addressing the growing and asymmetric nature of risks that permeate companies globally and frequently produce almost instantaneous adverse effects.

Reputation Risks Are A Fiduciary Responsibility

The management, stewardship, and oversight of most company's reputation risks are now characterized as legitimate and compelling fiduciary responsibilities. Consequently, reputation risk management practices should be factors at every operational level in a company: R&D, manufacturing, business transactions, new market-entry initiatives, etc. The objectives are to ensure company reputation risk management practices lead to achieving a reputation risk-intelligent company culture, and becoming a more reputation risk–resilient organization.

Achieving these states are fiduciary imperatives, not merely risk management luxuries that can be developed on-the-fly or after the fact to respond to an already materialized risk or threat event or act.

Building A Strong Business Case for Reputation Risk Management

As CSOs know well, most every security/risk management initiative must be accompanied by an equally strong business case typically describing the initiative's contributory value to the company along with identifying performance indicators along the way that warrant regular monitoring and assessment. These aspects are uniquely designed to serve the CSOs by, among other things, respectfully demonstrating a strong business return-on-security-investment (ROSI) case for companies to invest in and execute reputation risk management initiatives.

As such, any ROSI discussion should bring clarity to reputation risk management as a distinctive, rapid-acting, asymmetric, and potentially cascading category of risk; demonstrate practical monitoring and assessment tools, performance metrics, and timely alerts; and include key design and cost factors for the reputation risk management initiative.

For example, Dr. Nir Kossovsky (2010), President and CEO of Steel City Re, has developed a corporate reputation index that captures, in quantitative form, the consequences of companies' actions toward their stakeholders—that is, customers, employees, vendors, and investors. Companies with higher reputation rankings on the index produce higher equity returns and have lower credit costs, which in turn lead to lower operating costs and higher net incomes. Dr. Kossovsky 'uses four instruments to measure reputation which include the weekly Steel City Re Corporate Reputation Index ranks, the Fortune 50 Most Admired. The Forbes Most Reputable list and the Harris RQ list. While the latter three are reported once a year and are based on surveys and expert panel review, the Steel City Re Corporate Reputation Index is a periodic quantitative algorithm that captures the consequences of companies' actions toward their shareholders, including: Customers (sales, volume and revenue), Employees (employment terms, internal politics), Vendors (merchandise credit, operating terms and operating friction) and Investors (earnings multiples and price volatility).

An obvious and positive consequence is that in rising markets, shareholders of companies with superior reputation rankings are rewarded with higher returns. In down market cycles companies with superior reputations are found to be more resilient and lose less value should a reputation risk materialize.

NOT PUBLIC RELATIONS WITH A TWIST

Any presumption that company reputation risks merely constitute a thinly disguised and tweaked version of public relations is incorrect. As most have recognized over the past three to five years, there are far too many companies that have responded poorly or incorrectly to risks affecting their reputation.

Why is that? Management teams remain inclined to view the management of company reputation in still fairly narrow and conventional contexts that fall to the reactive public relation unit, some of which remain inclined to put fires out after the fact. Consequently, there are two key circumstances that companies with poorly developed reputation risk management capabilities: they permit reputation risks to be incorrectly assessed, and they fester and exacerbate to the point they actually trigger higher levels of risk crises that rapidly cascade internally and externally.

Such perspectives are certainly out-of-step with the 24/7 realities of global news and social media platforms, which are unforgiving and increasingly irreversible first-strike launching pads and spawning grounds for reputation risks to go viral. When any component of a company's reputation is not routinely being monitored and assessed for missteps, miscues, or external attacks, be they inadvertent or purposeful, most companies can anticipate consumer ill-feelings to be further aggravated and become deeper and broader than they may have initially had a company appropriately dealt with its inevitable reputation risks at the outset. More precisely, decision makers must correctly recognize, distinguish, and assess acts or events as reputation risks at their very earliest stages and rapidly set in motion genuine mitigation initiatives.

Reputation risk management is about being proactive, which requires having the capability to not only consistently monitor, but correctly distinguish and assess, the gravity of adverse acts, events, revelations, and statements (social media or otherwise) in the context of if or how they may affect consumer expectations. To reflect on the sage counsel of Warren Buffet: "It takes years to build a favorable company reputation, but today, company reputation can literally become severely damaged, if not irrevocably lost, in a single day" (http://www.goodreads.com/quotes/148174). I would further say that this could even come down to a matter of hours, not an entire day.

REPUTATION RISK EXAMPLE: CRAIG'S LIST

From a company reputation risk management perspective, the Craig's List situation during the fall of 2010 was not specifically sparked or orchestrated by a single interest group or blog blitz that went viral. Instead, the situation experienced by Craig's List was largely the outcome of their own making, virally festering for some time.

That is, the adverse reactions and underlying sentiments to permitting and retaining their adult-services section had been simmering above and below the surface for many months. I can only presume that Craig's List decision makers made repeated business decisions, prior to the September 4, 2010, adult-services section shutdown, to permit this section to continue to function more or less as-is, with its increasingly transparent and explicit content for sexual services.

Craig's List management teams may well have dismissed well-recognized reputation risk best practices. Some 15 states' attorney generals joined in a class-action suit against the Craig's List adult-services section, generally describing it as merely a "thinly veiled, web-based advertising platform for prostitution and an array of other sexual services" (PBS Newshour, 2010).

Among the many interesting aspects was their decision to not remove the adult-services section more quickly, which conceivably may have put the matter behind them. Instead, they opted to retain the adult-services section and presumably mitigate the adverse reactions by inserting the word "censored."

Admittedly, I have no insight into Craig's List's decision-making processes on this matter. The decision to use the word "censored" in this instance implied that a total suspension of the adult-services section may have been forthcoming. Or, perhaps, the word "censored" in this instance merely represents a temporary patch decision with a more permanent "fix" to the larger issue of sustaining or discontinuing the adult-services section still under consideration.

From afar, this was likely a circumstance in which a business orientation dominated a company's reputation risk management process that believed hedging the initial adverse reaction to their adult-services section would be temporary with no long-lasting reputation risk.

Factors Contributing to Reputation Risks

Dr. Daniel Diermeier, IBM Professor of Regulation and Competitive Practice at Northwestern University's Kellogg School of Management, and Harlan Loeb, Global Practice Chair, Edelman Crisis & Risk, Adjunct Professor, Northwestern University School of Law, identified four key factors that contribute to triggering increases in company reputation risks (Diermeier and Loeb, 2013):

1. Media coverage, whether traditional or social, which has increased dramatically worldwide, sparking increased scrutiny that companies simply can't avoid.
   a. Transparency is expected because once an issue is alive on the Internet it becomes permanent and facts become "negotiable."
2. Globalization of activist organizations now matches the global reach of companies; consequently, NGOs succeed in forcing private regulation.
   a. That is the "voluntary" adoption of rules and standards that constrain certain forms of company conduct without involving public agents.

   b. The mechanism driving much of the change proves to be the creation of reputational crises for global entities, which often force companies to change their business practices.

3. Expectations of corporate conduct have shifted, especially among younger demographic groups.

   a. This helps explain the explosive growth of corporate social responsibility, sustainability, and socially responsible investing.

   b. These aren't passing fads. Yet, increasingly, moral outrage drives reputational crises, whether over environmental concerns or executive perks.

4. Business models based on trust have emerged and are on the rise.

   a. Companies are recognizing that to develop unique customer experiences and solutions they must draw closer to their customers' unspoken—perhaps, even unconscious—desires and needs.

   b. This requires trust. While this shift generates fresh opportunities to create value, even the mere perception of broken trust produces strong feelings of betrayal. This proves a particular challenge for the banking industry, as today's headlines show.

While most corporate management teams are indeed more cognizant of issues that drive reputation risks, many, it appears, remain unsure about precisely what to do or who should do it. Yet still, numerous companies and their leadership teams cling to the view that forging a strong reputation is relatively easy in as much as it merely requires a common-sense approach to its customers, suppliers, stakeholders, and investors. To them, it is simply a natural consequence of doing what is right.

For them, a tutorial on social media and the direct evidence of how it has, in essence, changed the rules (conventional past practices) for effectively countering and mitigating the expense and potential irreversibility related to the materialization of reputation risks would be a prudent use of their time.

What the Public Is Saying

In most instances, a company's reputation rests on what the general public is saying about them. Thus, I encourage company officials, in their development of reputation risk best practices, to examine acts, events, and statements through the lens of the public's perspectives and viewpoints, especially when they're critical or hostile. A proper response by company management requires a strategic rather than strictly an offensive or defensive approach.

A strategic response requires company management teams to possess the emotional strength to treat reputational difficulties as being understandable, perhaps even being predictable challenges that, to some extent, should be expected in today's aggressive business transaction environments. Companies and chief executives must handle reputational crises like any other major business challenge: based on principled leadership and supported by sophisticated processes and capabilities that integrate with the company's business strategy and culture. Most every company's reputational trust depends on it.

Reputation Risks: The Most Difficult Risk Type for Companies to Manage

For readers who may be unfamiliar with The ACE Group, it purports to be one of the world's largest multiline property and casualty insurers for a diverse clientele with operations in 54 countries. In reviewing its 2013 report "Reputation at Risk" by Andrew Kendrick, the president of ACE's European Group, there are some revealing findings that broaden current thinking regarding reputation risk. So much so that business decision makers globally would be well served at minimum to read this entry, but also read ACE's entire report.

ACE's survey finds that merely 1 in 5 companies reported they are very effective at measuring external perceptions about their company. Almost 4 in 10 respondents also report their companies have confidence in their ability to address and recover from a crisis with 32% believing they are very effective at restoring reputation following the materialization of a risk event. I am skeptical about assuming crisis management and reputation risk management are synonymous. From an insurance perspective, two-thirds of ACE's survey respondents feel inadequately covered for reputational risk. So, one can presume the respondents distinguished crisis management from reputation risk management.

Most company management teams recognize, however, that the time that companies now have to respond should be factored in hours and minutes, thanks in large part to the globally instantaneous functionality of expanding numbers of social media platforms. One outcome of this particular reputation risk phenomena is that fewer companies have the luxury of a second chance.

There Are no Magic Solutions to Manage Reputation Risk

There are some things that companies can do to mitigate, if not prevent, the materialization of reputation risks, though there is no magic solution. A couple of effective measures that business management teams should execute include:

- Do more to evaluate and systematically track the perceptions of primary external stakeholders, such as customers, media, adverse lobbying groups, and governmental regulators.

- Help these entities acquire true perspectives and insights into challenging trends and problems companies face.

Better preparation and routine testing of response plans builds an important foundation for a faster, more effective, and genuine response when reputation risks materialize, including for reputation restoration in the instantaneously global social media network.

Communicating Risk and Clarifying A Company's Appetite for Risk

Companies and organizations encounter risk every day, even multiple times per day. It's absolutely critical that intangible asset strategists, when working with a company, recognize and respect that just because key business unit and management team members are at the same table, seldom do their perceptions and targets of risk coincide nor is consensus easily reached.

This is due in large part to another reality, which is a sizable number of management teams, while they may generally know what intangible assets are, they remain operationally unfamiliar with the ones their company produces and utilizes, and they have yet to feel compelled to achieve a higher level of operational familiarity to consistently engage their intangible assets more effectively, competitively, and profitably. Obviously, these realities present some challenges. One is that it can impair the accuracy of a company's risk assessment.

A significant percentage of economic adversaries globally are really seeking a company's intellectual, structural, and relationship capital—that is, their intangible assets. Therefore, it is these intangible assets that management teams are obliged to address and mitigate risks to, which starts by communicating what those risks are, and putting in place practices, policies, and procedures designed to simultaneously sustain control, use, ownership, and monitor the assets' value, materiality, and risks. That is, if a company is to maintain its path of success, profitability, and competitive positioning.

However, a fundamental question remains: How much risk does a company's decision makers find acceptable as they pursue their company's mission and objectives? In other words, what is their "appetite" for risk?

A complicating factor to answering the question lies in the reality that regulators, various oversight entities, and certainly stakeholders are seeking, if not demanding, companies develop better descriptions of their risk management processes. The Committee of Sponsoring Organizations of the Treadway Commission (COSO, 2012) suggests that communicating company risk should commence by understanding how much risk a company is willing to accept. And, to what extent should the risks that a company accepts mirror stakeholders' objectives and attitudes toward risk? Does a company ensure that its business units are operating within the agreed-on boundaries that actually represent the company's appetite for specific kinds of risk?

COSO (2012) defines *risk appetite* as the amount of risk a company is willing to accept in pursuit of value. Each company pursues various objectives to add value and should recognize and understand the risks it is willing to undertake to achieve those objectives. Therefore, the answers to the preceding questions essentially frame a company's risk appetite.

Therefore, risk management decision making and compliance should not be executed as if they were separate and distinct from strategic planning and daily decision making. Rather, both should be recognized as important components to a company's culture, just as making decisions to attain a company's business initiatives, projects, and objectives should be part of a company's culture.

As a company and its management teams actually begin to factor their risk appetite into their decision-making processes, they will become better positioned to balance business risks with business opportunities. For example, if a CEO expressed a need or desire to increase his or her company's risk appetite based on expectations that key aspects of its profitability were declining or would become stagnant, it's quite likely, if it were a:

- Financial services firm, by accepting a lower risk appetite, it may well choose to avoid opportunities that produce higher levels of risk while offering the possibility of higher returns.
- Manufacturing firm that accepts a higher appetite for risk it may be more inclined to engage an opportunity to procure natural resources from a volatile country where its investment could be lost, literally at the whim of that country's political leaders. Obviously, in this instance the rewards may be high, but the risks are high as well.

So, company decision makers are obliged, if not fiduciarily responsible, to consider their risk appetite in unison with their company's goals and selecting which operational tactics to pursue.

References

Bonime-Blanc, A., 2013. The Global Ethicist – Risky Business. <http://www.ethicalcorp.com/business-strategy/globalethicist-%E2%80%93-risky-business> (accessed 7 May 2014).

COSO, 2012. The Committee of Sponsoring Organizations of the Treadway Commission. Enterprise Risk Management: Understanding and Communicating Risk Appetite by Martens, F. and Rittenberg, L. Durham, NC.

Diermeier, D., Loeb, H., 2013. Reputation Risk Management—It's time to Build Trust and Resilience at the Top. <http://www.huffingtonpost.com/daniel-diermeier/reputation-risk-managemen_b_3253498.html> (accessed 7 May 2014).

Eccles, R., Newquist, S., Schatz, R., February 2007. Reputation and its Risks' Harvard Business Review.

Kendrick, A., 2013. Reputation at Risk. Report of the ACE's European Group. London, UK.

Kossovsky, N., 2010. Mission Intangible: Managing Risk and Reputation To Create Enterprise Value. Intangible Asset Finance Society in association with Trafford Publishing, Pittsburgh, PA.

Resnick, J., 2006. Reputational Risk Management: A Framework for Safeguarding Your Organization's Primary Asset, Princeton, NJ.

Distinguishing Intellectual Property and Intangible Assets

Over the past 25 years I have made countless speeches, presentations, conducted seminars, and participated in business meetings with a wide array of professionals and practitioners representing most every industry sector. In each, I am asked to address the terms *intangible assets* and *intellectual property*. In that regard, I know of no study to support what I am about to say, nor do I know of any study that would refute it either. That is, if one were to randomly engage 10 people on a global main street and ask them to explain or give examples of intellectual property, I guesstimate the following would likely occur:

■ Five individuals would use the word "patent" only to describe intellectual property (IP), probably absent any reference or connection to other forms of IP such as trademarks, copyrights, or trade secrets.

■ Five individuals would likely admit they had no familiarity with IP conceptually, practically, or operationally.

It may be fair to infer from these guesstimates that large segments of business leaders and management teams remain unnecessarily and operationally unfamiliar with their intangible assets and IP in terms of

- What intangible assets are and what they're not.
- Their potential value and revenue-producing capabilities.
- How to effectively identify, utilize, exploit, and profit from the intangible assets their business produces, particularly the intellectual, relationship, and structural capital.
- IP is actually one type of intangible asset.

Recall that more than 80% of most companies' value, sources of revenue, and building blocks for growth, sustainability, and profitability actually evolve directly from intangible assets. Based on this irreversible and steadily rising global economic fact, business management teams have a professional responsibility to achieve operational familiarity with intangible assets and their distinguishing and contributory elements.

Patents Are Intangible Assets Suitable for Framing

Intellectual property—that is, patents, trademarks, copyrights, etc.—is merely one type of intangible asset. The only substantive distinction between IP and intangible assets is that IP is applied for and issued by the U.S. Patent and Trademark Office (USPTO), whereas intangible assets are not.

Once IP has been issued by the USPTO, it assumes a sense of physicality (tangibility)—that is, a patent certificate can be framed and hung on an office wall as a testament to one's hard and long periods of intense and diligent intellectual work. However, there are no accompanying documents that convey the valuable intangible assets that exist within the IP.

It is these embedded intangible assets that, when effectively exploited, can collectively pave the way for infringers to achieve the sought-after revenue, competitive advantage, branding, and reputation enhancements. Frequently, IP, particularly patents, represents a presumptive "brass ring" that a significant percentage of technology transfer units, researchers, inventors, business management teams, and legal counsel set their sights on.

Patent-Only Strategy

Being fortunate enough to having a patent issued represents a very worthy culmination of one's work and is a genuine testament to perseverance and intellectual acuity. However, a business that engages in a patent-only strategy to protect their IP may be reflective of the reality that the parties are unfamiliar with the necessary preparatory aspects that skilled intangible asset strategists can contribute; instead, they opt to only engage IP legal counsel. An intangible asset strategist can articulate equally relevant options for optimizing, commercializing, and monetizing intangible assets that are frequently complimentary to conventional IP strategies.

Being fixated on a patent-only strategy, business management teams may overlook, undervalue, and project somewhat of a dismissive attitude toward the contributory intangible assets embedded in every patent application. Those attitudes are often rooted in the convention that an issued patent singularly conveys ownership, certain rights, and provides legal standing for asset defensibility under the law.

However, the legal and administrative costs associated with obtaining and maintaining a patent are not insignificant, not to mention the extraordinary costs necessary to pursue infringers and counterfeiters or to defend a patent against allegations of infringement. These costs continue to escalate, making the patent-only tract increasingly out-of-reach for a frugal innovator or SME (small- or medium-size enterprise) absent securing highly committed investors with very deep pockets.

Deterrence

Under ideal circumstances, the probability of getting caught, becoming a defendant to a lawsuit, paying a hefty fine or legal fees, or receiving a prison sentence would be sufficient to deter infringement. This concept of deterrence is what many patent applicants misunderstand, naïvely accept, or are unwittingly being oversold. Deterrence is not a simple concept and should not be conveyed as if it were. There are many factors—human, economic, cultural, and environmental—that are applicable to achieving some manner of desired deterrent effect.

To genuinely achieve any deterrent effect is a challenging undertaking and should not be assumed is a naturally occurring outcome of having a patent issued. The reality is patents simply do not constitute an adequate inhibitor to infringers who believe the shortest path to success is to acquire someone else's know-how.

The misperception that patents are companies' only option or strategy to optimize and exploit their intellectual and structural capital can lead to substantial disappointments for inventors, innovators, and entrepreneurs. These disappointments, while they may not be totally avoided, can certainly be mitigated with more effective deterrents.

Throughout my encounters with countless private and academic researchers representing a broad spectrum of entrepreneurism from extraordinary biotech to less sophisticated, but nevertheless useful apps, I have found there are commonalities among researchers and entrepreneurs, especially in attitudes and behaviors, such as:

- They possess substantial optimism about projections for achieving lucrative outcomes from the commercialization and monetization of their innovation.
- They are unwittingly naïve about the necessity that even issued patents warrant management, oversight, and stewardship; and the necessity to have practices in place designed specifically to sustain control, use, and ownership, and monitor value, materiality, and risk.
- They are eager to share oftentimes intimate details of their innovation story.
- They possess highly opinionated knowledge and familiarity regarding other relevant innovation/research projects occurring globally.

Therefore, entrepreneurs and management teams electing to effectively and consistently engage their intangible assets in a regime of stewardship, oversight, and management will certainly improve the odds that their innovation will come to fruition.

The Shortest and Least Expensive Path to Success Is Infringement

There is a well-used adage in the asset protection arena that is particularly apropos to intangible asset strategists and information asset protection practitioners: The shortest path to innovation/invention commercialization and monetization does not always lie in incurring the substantial time, resources, and costs associated with conventional (legal, ethical) R&D models. Instead, it lies in illegally acquiring the necessary data, information, intellectual and structural capital, or prototypes from the rightful asset holders and producing the product in an illegal manner, known as product counterfeiting, and inserting the counterfeits in legitimate supply chains globally.

There are important asset preparations that should occur prior to launching any new innovation, product, or service, or handing off intellectual and structural intangible assets to IP/patent counsel. Examples of these preparations evolve around ensuring that companies have procedures and practices in place designed specifically to safeguard and monitor the assets' value, materiality, and prevent or mitigate risk.

What Is Your IP Position?

It remains true that prospective investors, venture capitalists, and large multinational corporations that express interest in an individual inventor's or company's research product, as well as those who may be fortunate enough to "pitch" their innovation at a well-attended venture forum, are inclined to believe the "What is your IP position" question directed to the inventor or innovator remains as relevant today as it did in the 1960s.

Sure, patent enforcement tools, conveyed by virtue of having an issued patent, are important and will likely remain offensive and defensive mainstays for the foreseeable future.

Having attended numerous venture forums myself, without exception, every entrepreneur in their presentation to the venture capitalists in the audience felt it was necessary to clarify their IP position at some point during their presentation. So it comes as no surprise that being unable to respond affirmatively to the question is a nonstarter for most venture capitalists and other categories of investors. From an entrepreneur's perspective, having no patent issued nor having submitted a provisional patent application are often assumed to be the death knell for attracting much needed investment.

However, the absence of an IP position does not necessarily have to be a dealbreaker for prospective investors, providing the entrepreneur has acquired sufficient operational familiarity with and can articulate the numerous contributing intangible assets and how their firm has effective asset stewardship, oversight, and management practices in place to sustain control, use, and ownership of the assets, and monitor their value, materiality, and risk.

An Analogy

When a business owner seeks the guidance of a search engine optimization (SEO) or website design/marketing firm, it's routine to hear the firm's business development or marketing persons' opening pitch to include some variation of "We will help you get your company website and/or blog on page one of Google!" Of course, the reality is, there is absolutely no guarantee such claims will come to fruition. But, with virtually no exceptions, each firm I have encountered makes some variation of that claim.

Therefore, there are two important things people should know and sort out for themselves:

- There are countless books, webinars, and one-on-one coaching available to help people repeatedly integrate language in their web design copy to achieve the coveted high ranking on Google or other prominent search engine. Typically, such claims flow from their presumed understanding of and ability to favorably influence the famed "Google algorithms."
- Getting one's business website or blog on page one of Google is no guarantee it will produce the all-important conversions that SEO marketers routinely tout.

Yes, entrepreneurs and businesses can rationalize that all it takes is one good conversion to kick-start a company down the path to riches. We all wish that were true and envy those for whom it materializes in that manner. But, "reaching page one of Google" by itself is certainly not all that a company needs as a requisite for achieving success.

A well-coordinated, focused, and specific strategy effectively utilizes an array of Internet resources and social media platforms that present many different options to elevate a company's exposure and conversion rates, not solely landing on page one of Google! Similarly, pursuing a patent-only strategy may not, in all circumstances, be the best option.

Getting An Invention Business Ready

For companies that are seeking strategies to get their inventions business ready in 2014 and beyond it may be more prudent for their first contact to be with an intangible asset strategist rather than IP legal counsel. Among the multiple roles this strategist would undertake are to identify, unravel, and assess the origins, status, stability, and defensibility of the intangible assets they have produced that underlie every innovation. The intangible asset strategist would describe strategies that fit best and work best for the innovator or company.

This makes achieving a fundamental operational familiarity with intangible assets aside from conventional intellectual properties an increasingly essential prelude for achieving business success, which includes building and sustaining a strong and sustainable internal pipeline of intellectual, structural, and relationship capital to achieve business aspirations.

Trade Secrets Start Life as Intellectual Capital

Trade secrets are merely another form or category of intangible asset, specifically intellectual capital. A ruling by the U.S. District Court (Northern District of California) may serve as an impetus for entrepreneurs and innovation-intensive companies to engage intangible asset strategists first, and IP counsel second, to ensure agreements they have entered into as well as company policies, procedures, and practices duly reflect the perspective that all trade secrets start life as intellectual capital.

On June 7, 2012, in *Form Factor, Inc. v. Micro-Probe, Inc.*, the U.S. District Court's ruling brought clarity to the evidentiary requisites to support an allegation of trade secret theft. The Court record states that an employee (defendant) left Form Factor to work for Micro-Probe, a competitor, a circumstance that most readers know occurs routinely. These two firms were clearly competitive rivals. Both sold and provided support services for similar products used to test the performance of semi-conductors. While the companies did have some overlapping customer relationships, their products actually conducted different kinds of semi-conductor performance tests according to court statements.

While employed by Form Factor, the defendant (former employee) had been authorized to remotely access the employer's internal network through a laptop provided by his employer, and his personal home computer. When the defendant informed his employer (Form Factor) he was leaving to work for Micro-Probe, he dutifully returned his company-owned laptop as required. Unfortunately, however, according to court records, Form Factor made three significant errors (omissions) with respect to their now former employee: they made no inquiries about whether the defendant retained any proprietary data/information files on his personal computer; they did not request that the defendant return or delete any proprietary materials that he had downloaded while working from home on either computer; and the defendant never signed any restrictive nondisclosure or noncompete agreement.

However, shortly after the defendant formally left Form Factor, at Form Factor's request, the defendant relinquished his personal computer and other data storage devices for inspection by Form Factor personnel to determine if either contained trade secrets or confidential information.

Form Factor's inspection revealed the presence of approximately 4500 files that remained stored on the defendant's personal computer and its storage devices, all of which were the property of Form Factor. However, following the inspection and comparing it to Micro-Probe's databases and electronic data/information storage system, only 1 of those 4500 files appeared in Micro-Probe's possession.

Consequently, the Court noted that any party seeking recovery under California's Uniform Trade Secrets Act for alleged acts of misappropriation (in this instance, FormFactor) must demonstrate the existence of a trade secret, must identify the trade secret, and must carry the burden of showing that the trade secret actually exists.

Helping to further collapse Form Factor's claim was that, of the 4500 files found on the defendant's personal computer, none met the requisites of trade secrecy. Thus, the blanket assertion that all of the files were confidential or contained a trade secret was rejected outright by the Court.

In addition, the Court ruled that Form Factor, to add legitimacy to their claims, were required to identify each specific trade secret, not just a broad statement that a file might contain a trade secret; describe the subject matter of each trade secret; and establish that each alleged trade secret met the six requisites of trade secrecy, particularly that each held independent economic value.

The requisites are as follows:

- The extent to which the information is known outside the claimant's business.
- The extent to which it is known by employees and others involved in the business.
- The extent of measures taken by the claimant to guard the secrecy of the information.
- The value of the information to the business and its competitors.

- The amount of effort or money expended by the business in developing the information.
- The ease or difficulty with which the information could be properly acquired or duplicated by others.

It should come as no surprise for experienced practitioners that requiring plaintiffs to disclose trade secrets in open court will surely give companies pause about pursuing trade secret theft claims.

Also, the Court presented Form Factor with yet another embarrassment by stating that their broad argument that they spent $50 million annually on R&D was insufficient for establishing a legitimate connection between the value of the contested trade secret on the defendant's personal computer and Form Factor's level of annual R&D expenditures.

Lastly, the Court held Form Factor had not demonstrated reasonable efforts were in place to safeguard the alleged trade secret—that is, they never required the defendant to sign a confidentiality or nondisclosure agreement, which allowed the defendant to retain his contact information (relationship capital) after his departure from Form Factor, and authorized the defendant and other employees to work from home and access the company's proprietary data/information bases. They also did not request the defendant return any FormFactor data/information upon tendering his resignation.

Ultimately, Form Factor did not establish the existence of any protectable trade secrets, nor did they establish misappropriation—that is, improper acquisition or use—of its trade secrets had actually occurred, at least under California's Uniform Trade Secrets Act. Mere possession of an alleged trade secret by a departing employee, standing alone, does not presume misappropriation.

In addition, the single file that the defendant took to his new employer, Micro-Probe, was actually a spreadsheet that contained information that had not been identified (by Form Factor) as being either confidential or proprietary in nature. This single file being contested was constructed in a format that was common to the industry and therefore was not deemed unique to Form Factor. Plus, there was no evidence that Micro-Probe ever actually used that document's content.

Given the extraordinary growth of knowledge-intensive companies globally, this ruling should serve as yet one more testament to how companies, particularly entrepreneurial firms, and their management teams should acquire operational familiarity with and give favorable consideration to strictly following the six requisites of trade secrecy.

McAfee's IP Theft Report

I am, in no way, advocating a protectionist view with respect to intangible assets or IP. I am, however, a strong proponent of Article I, Section 8 of the U.S. Constitution that states that if someone invents a new product and/or technology, and has been issued a patent, trademark, or copyright by the USPTO, only they should reap the economic and competitive-advantage benefits from their efforts.

For those fortunate enough to have an issued IP, they assume the sole responsibility for sustaining the exclusivity of their innovation, effectively safeguard their proprietary intangible assets and IP, and consistently monitor and aggressively pursue any and all suspicions of misappropriation, infringement, compromise, or theft. Of course, each is frequently dependent on numerous variables, not the least of which are resources, recognition of the need, and sufficient operational familiarity with intangible assets to distinguish the intellectual and structural capital that should remain proprietary. Also, it is essential to recognize not all countries or cultures interpret or embrace the western-dominated perspectives of IP exclusivity or its protections in the same manner.

For example, in 2009, McAfee published a report that showed if an enterprise (country, company, organization, etc.) can illegally appropriate R&D, for example, at minimal cost and then go on to produce a comparable product (albeit a counterfeited product developed from infringed IP) at a far lower cost, basic economics suggest that the manufacturer of the infringed product will win space in the marketplace.

Thus, the incentives for state-sponsored entities, companies, or individuals to engage in industrial and economic espionage and otherwise appropriate others' proprietary intangible assets and IP remains high, particularly in markets (countries) where there are few, if any, well-established brands and corresponding consumer brand loyalty, and there is an abundance of legacy-free players (Friedman, 2007) in which private property ownership remains a relatively new concept as does the ownership of IP.

To deter these action, it's absolutely essential today that:

- There is an ongoing dialogue among a company's various professional and functional disciplines regarding intangible assets.
- Each business discipline's perspective of intangible asset risk is recognized and respected.
- A consensus is reached on what actions (policies, procedures, practices, etc.) are necessary to prevent, deter, and mitigate the identified risks and vulnerabilities.

Nine Reasons for Implementing Intangible Asset Safeguards

There are nine reasons a company should implement intangible asset safeguards now:

1. Perhaps foremost, more than 80% of most companies' value and sources of revenue evolve from intangible assets.

2. Conventional forms of IP ownership and enforcement (patents, particularly) are no longer stand-alone deterrents, nor are they synonymous with sustaining control, use, or ownership of those assets or the ability to reap rightfully owned and hard-earned economic and competitive-advantage benefits.

3. Intangible assets, in most forms, are perishable and often nonrenewable, and when compromised, full recovery (value) is seldom achieved.

4. The long-held perspectives that the stewardship, oversight, and management responsibilities associated with intangible assets have traditionally been portrayed as legal or accounting processes now warrant reframing as business and strategic planning decisions.

5. The timeframe when companies should expect the most value from their intangible assets relative to their respective life cycle continues to be compressed, in no small part due to lower barriers to market space entry and the significant and rapid profits achieved from large-scale and globally organized counterfeiting operations that routinely become embedded in legitimate supply chains.

6. The growing global universality of regulatory mandates regarding reporting, accounting, and materiality changes related to intangible assets.

7. The value of key intangible assets is more fragile than business decision makers should assume, thus when compromised, economic and competitive-advantage market space hemorrhaging can commence rapidly.

8. Global data mining and business intelligence operations contribute to asset compromises through aggressive and economically and culturally embedded intelligence collection and analysis to rapidly undermine asset value and counter a company's strategic planning and competitive advantages at the earliest stages of their development.

9. Intangible assets must be less about how to measure them and more about determining what assets to measure, distinguishing which assets carry valuable proprietary elements and competitive advantages, and the contributory elements of the assets.

Intellectual Property

IP is an original creative work that can be protected by law as a patent, copyright, or trademark. In exchange for exclusive protections for a specified period of time, the holder must disclose their IP as prelude to enable other companies, innovators, and competitors to recreate the works upon its expiration. Otherwise (granted through Article 1, Section 8, Clause 8 of the U.S. Constitution and its comparables in other countries), it would be much easier for others to "steal" ideas or use ideas without compensating the rightful holder.

PATIENTS

The U.S. Constitution establishes the right to patent or copyright a work through Congress' power "to promote the Progress of Science and useful Arts, by securing, again for limited periods of time, to authors and inventors the exclusive right to their respective writings and discoveries" (U.S. Constitution, Article 1, Section 8, Clause 8).

The issuance of a patent gives the inventor the legal right "to exclude others from making, using, offering for sale, or selling the invention throughout the United States or importing the invention into the United States" for a limited period of time, again, in exchange for public disclosure of the invention when the patent is granted (35 USC 154; USPTO). Again, it's the responsibility of the holder of the patent to enforce these rights.

COPYRIGHT

Copyright is automatically granted at the "moment a (written) work is created and fixed in a tangible form either directly perceivable or through a machine or device" (*www.copyright.gov*). Because a copyright is instantly created as soon as work is put into a tangible form, the individual doing so generally becomes the initial owner of the copyright unless a company has other policies and procedures already in place that stipulate otherwise. A copyright notice (e.g., © 2014 John Doe) is not a requirement to serve as notice of copyright ownership; however, it is beneficial and encouraged for putting potential infringers on notice.

However, if an author believes his or her copyrighted material will be coveted by others and therefore may be subject to being copied or infringed without permission, then the author would be prudent to register the copyright ahead of pursuing litigation. It's important to recognize that an employee would not likely register a copyright independently, because copyright ownership may instead fall to an employer. Each company may have their own policy and practices on copyrighting employee-authored papers.

Registration of a copyright makes it part of the public record, which can allow for recovery of damages and attorney's fees should infringement of copyright be proven through litigation. These benefits may not be of interest to all, but companies are encouraged to consider how or if copyrights are applicable to internally developed work, such as training manuals. Copyright registration can be done anytime; there are no time constraints as there are in filing patents.

OWNERSHIP OF INVENTIONS AND COMPANY IP POLICY

An employee or researcher is considered an inventor of an issued patent if at least one claim in the issued patent has been conceived by him or her. Inventorship and authorship are distinctive and often confused. Occasionally ownership of inventions becomes a contentious issue. When this occurs, it makes it all the more important for companies to have well-designed policies that fully explain these issues and describe specifically how ownership is established.

An inventor is sometimes different than someone who may be included or identified as an author or coauthor, particularly in scholarly publications. To be classified as an inventor requires a factual analysis of each person's actual contribution to a specific invention (Stewart and Jenkins, 2009).

With respect to patents, the inventor is the initial legal owner. Ownership of a patent by the inventor's employer comes through an assignment of the patent's ownership rights by the inventor (White, 2009). For example, researchers in a company's R&D unit may remain the inventor, but the ownership rights are transferred to their employer as an assignment.

A company's IP policy may require assignment of all inventions related to work conducted by an employee researcher. Each employee researcher is always advised to become informed about the specifics of their employer's policies on IP. In most instances, however, they are agreed to upon employment as part of their employment contract.

There are cases of joint inventors—that is, employees of the same company contribute to an invention through a collaboration for which each has an undivided interest or legal right to the entire patent (Burmania, 2009). There can also be co-inventors to an invention who happen to be employed by different, but generally allied, companies as a strategic alliance or research consortium. The companies will have entered into an intercompany agreement to manage the invention and delegate responsibilities for patenting and licensing in advance (Burmania, 2009). Co-inventions will likely become more common, if not a norm in certain industry sectors. As such occurrences continue to evolve, companies engaging in such strategic (R&D) alliances or consortiums will also find it prudent to negotiate, reach consensus, and describe contractually and with relevant specificity, key elements in order to reduce the probability that subsequent disputes or challenges will arise.

A company's IP policy should also describe all circumstances when a company can assume ownership of copyrighted materials as well as circumstances when copyright ownership can remain with the author. The creative initiative, control of content, and any extra compensation by the employer to an employee will be factors a company should take into consideration when developing their IP policies, with special attention to determining ownership of copyrightable material (CSU, 2003).

Also, each company may have different requirements or restrictions, stated in their IP policy, relative to the rights to and use of technical data and software developed under a particular research project by employees (Hardy, n.d.).

PUBLIC DISCLOSURE

It is important that all employees understand how premature public disclosure can adversely affect novelty under patent law (Massey Licata, 2009). The ability to receive a patent for an invention can be adversely affected if public disclosure occurs prior to filing a patent application. Public disclosure occurs when someone of "ordinary skill in the art" (The University of Kansas, n.d.) can determine the key aspects of an invention without having direct access to any proprietary information or content related to the invention. For definition purposes, public disclosure can include, among other similar acts, a presentation, publication, or discussion with individuals outside the confines of an inventor's company, such as with acquaintances, company representatives, or colleagues at a professional conference.

The following is important for company researchers, inventors, and R&D units to keep in mind relative to those who might be sharing information and receiving information. Discussions about an invention with colleagues, employees, lab assistants, and other personnel within the same organization or company would generally not be considered as constituting public disclosure. However, discussions with individuals outside (not employed by) the company who could be considered as possessing ordinary skill in the art (i.e., related to the invention and/or research) would likely, in most instances, constitute public disclosure.

It's both prudent and necessary for company researchers to treat discussions within their own company as confidential. Consistent adherence to this practice inhibits the inadvertent disclosure of proprietary information related to an invention or research project before it's under proper safeguards.

In the United States there is a one-year "grace period" the time an invention is publically disclosed to when a patent application must be filed. This "grace period" is derived from the novelty of patentability and is set forth in 35 USC § 102. It states that a patent cannot be obtained if the invention was already patented, determined to be publicly disclosed, or publicly used or sold more than one year before submitting the application for the current patent. It does not matter if the disclosure or use was by the present inventor. This grace period does not exist in any other country except the United States. In most countries any form of publication prior to making application for a patent will constitute a bar to patenting (Massey Licata, 2009). In most countries a patent application must be filed before public disclosure of an invention; otherwise, the invention will no longer be patentable.

PATENTABILITY EVALUATION

Because patents are expensive to prosecute and most companies have limited patent budgets, in most instances, companies will make an initial decision regarding the patentability of the invention (Nelson, 2007). When examining the patentability of an invention, most companies will take into consideration:

- Public disclosure
- Publications and patents (prior art)
- The state of the technology
- Potential claims that are broad enough to protect a future product or product line instead of a mere variation of an existing technology
- The ability to enforce the patent

Inventions originating in company R&D units generally constitute what is called applied research. Most adversaries are quite capable of examining applied research to predict what products will ultimately derive, and patent protection will likely be sought as being the most appropriate.

In most instances, the broader the scope of a patent's claims, the more marketable an invention will be and the more likely it will attract prospective investors or licensees, providing, of course, that is the strategy a company wishes to pursue. On the other hand, narrow patent claims elevate the probability that competitors will find it beneficial to try to design around the patent, thereby rendering it less attractive to prospective investors or licensees. Ultimately, if it's determined an abundance of information already exists relevant to the invention, this circumstance may lead to challenges obtaining a patent with sufficient strength and breadth of a company's desired claims.

Another important factor a company will consider during an invention's assessment and evaluation process is if or how the patent will be enforceable in terms of the ease or difficulty to detect infringement, misappropriation, compromises, counterfeiting, etc. Company decision makers should also be evaluating their innovation and inventions as to whether a patent-only strategy will be the most effective as a means to facilitate getting an invention to the market place.

Some aspects of invention determination strategies are dependent on a company's industry sector, the pace of change within that sector, and new product receptivity to consumer whims. The importance of these aspects can elevate substantially if the industry sector, as a whole, is already engaged in social media and distribution chains to developing countries in which competing industries exist, expanding economic development or benefits to specific groups.

CONFIDENTIALITY AND NONDISCLOSURE AGREEMENTS

A confidentiality agreement (CA) or nondisclosure agreement (NDA) are terms of employees and other relevant parties' interactions with a company to allow them to come in contact with proprietary elements but they are required to keep designated company-specific information confidential. These signatories to a CA or NDA are not permitted to disclose, as stipulated in the agreement's language, any information about company research, inventions, or other information designated as proprietary or a trade secret for a specified period of time.

A CA or NDA can be framed in one of two ways: a one-way or two-way agreement. A one-way agreement is the preferred method, particularly during the initial R&D and related discussions with colleagues and superiors and, eventually, with prospective buyers, licensees, or investors. Employees are required to keep the information confidential. A two-way agreement put the responsibility of confidentiality on both parties.

With most CAs and NDAs, there are specific provisions describing how any confidential information and materials received or exchanged must be handled. When CAs or NDAs are in effect, it's prudent that any exchanged documents be clearly marked with the word "confidential." It is also good practice when there is a verbal communication between parties to create a written summary of the exchange and mark those documents.

Islamic Law and Intellectual Property

Most other developed countries' IP laws, such as India, Brazil, European Union, China, Russia, Canada, are quite closely aligned with the principles and guidelines set forth by the WTO (World Trade Organization) as a requisite to gaining WTO membership. Islamic IP law, in comparison, has some distinctive features, some of which remain somewhat ambiguous with respect to religious interpretation.

It's certainly not an overly exaggerated vision to expect more western law firms will be establishing additional full-service offices in key business centers throughout the Muslim world, thereby relying less on in-country firms. There is growing evidence in some Islamic countries, particularly as certain employment, work, and trade-related conventions are relaxed, that their economies will become increasingly dependent on a broader array of intangible assets. Recognition of these assets will contribute to building, enhancing, and sustaining trade and business transactions on more of a global versus regional basis. And, one can expect, as these economies evolve and become more competitively aggressive in various industry sectors, challenges and disputes will surely arise.

In the next two to five years, business decision makers and transaction management teams globally will be jostling and competing for relevant information about operational aspects about the application of Islamic IP law, and Islamic countries will expect nothing less. Admittedly, I am not an expert in Islamic law, particularly those aspects that pertain to IP and other intangible assets. After reading and studying numerous, primarily academic, papers on this emerging business necessity, I defer to an excellent paper by Silvia Beltrametti (2010) to reference the material in this section.

Beltrametti states that IP rights are not regulated by Islamic law and its jurisprudence. Rather, the question or issue is whether the principles of Islamic law can be construed in a manner that actually provides for or supports IP right protections in a conventional context.

Beltrametti points out that challenges remain between the predominantly western and Islamic perspectives regarding IP rights, as well as the role economics plays within Islamic law and society. Beltrametti offers an intriguing suggestion in which an Islamic law-based legal and IP rights system is flexible and adaptable.

Another equally informative paper by Chad Cullen provides additional insight and is certainly worthy of one's time to read and study. Both authors:

- Agree that IP rights are not a particularly new concept to Islamic law. Some IP rights are actually strengthened by Islamic law, while others were never explicitly formulated as law; instead, they evolved as accepted social norms.
- Point out that since the advent of Islam, the concept of IP rights has expanded to include trademarks, patents, and certain forms of copyright by granting limited exclusive rights to works, in exchange for the commercialization of original creations that benefit society, while also allowing the owner to stop unauthorized use.
- Agree that Islamic law does not refer to Islamic legal rules only; rather, it encompasses a timeless concept of justice and fairness that may be best understood as constituting a higher rule of law with a divine connection.

After reviewing these and other sources, I concluded that:

- There are varying degrees of latitude with interpreting and applying IP and intangible asset matters under Islamic law.
- Such laws are not being aggressively enforced, at least at the present time. Infringement and misappropriation in the Middle East contributes to substantial losses of revenue for companies and individual business persons who are dependent on IP rights.

It's important to point out that such transgressions pose significant problems globally, not just in countries that practice Islamic law. Both Cullen and Beltrametti note, however, that an Islamic World Trade Organization member state is obligated to uphold the requirements of Trade Related Aspects of Intellectual Property Rights (TRIPS). This has led many Islamic states to enact IP laws that meet the minimum standards of TRIPS.

TRIPS is an international agreement administered by the WTO that sets down minimum standards for many forms of IP regulation as applied to nationals of other WTO members. TRIPS was negotiated at the end of the Uruguay Round of the General Agreement on Tariffs and Trade (GATT) in 1994.

The TRIPS agreement introduced IP law into the international trading system for the first time and remains the most comprehensive international agreement on IP to date. In 2001, developing countries, concerned that developed countries were insisting on an overly narrow reading of TRIPS, initiated a round of talks that resulted in the Doha Declaration, which is a WTO statement that clarifies the scope of TRIPS. Specifically, TRIPS requires WTO members to provide rights covering content producers, including performers, producers of sound recordings, and broadcasting organizations, that include appellations of origin and dispute resolution procedures.

In practice, however, IP rights have not been particularly well-received in some Islamic states. That is, a percentage of the Islamic community believe the concept of IP and the associated rights and responsibilities, particularly for IP-based innovations associated with advanced technologies, originate predominantly in the West, and not from their religious sources.

That said, numerous Islamic states have stringent IP laws and regulations in place. However, some remain ineffective or experience particular challenges related to actual enforcement of these rights. One question to pursue further then is whether this is a government-influenced choice or mandate, or an enforcement resource issue? Taking this perspective several steps further, some assume that forcing WTO membership and TRIPS upon Islamic states through threats of import/export restrictions and high tariffs underlie a perception that IP law, with provisions for the enforcement of IP rights, constitutes another facet or form of western oppression.

References

Akerman et al., 2009. Unsecured Economies Report: Protecting Vital Information. McAfee, Inc.: Santa Clara, CA.

Beltrametti, S., 2010. In: Mach, T. et al. (Eds). The Legality of Intellectual Property Rights Under Islamic Law. Anglo American University, Prague, pp. 55–94.

Burmania, J., 2009. Identifying and managing joint invention, Association of University Technology Managers Technology Transfer Manual: Managing the Invention Disclosure, Review and Protection Processes, third ed., vol. 3.

California State University (CSU), March, 2003. Intellectual Property, Fair Use, and the Unbundling of Ownership Rights, Part III, Section 1, p. 57.

Cullen, C.M., 2010. Can TRIPS live in Harmony with Islamic Law? An investigation of the relationship between intellectual property and Islamic Law. SMU Sci. Technol. Law Rev. Southern Methodist Dedman School of Law: Dallas, TX.

FormFactor, Inc. v. Micro-Probe, Inc., et al., No. C 10-3095 PJH, 2012 WL 2061520.N.D. Cal. June 7, 2012.

Friedman, T., 2007. 'The World Is Flat' 3.0: A Brief History of the Twenty-first Century, third ed. Picador.

Hardy, R., n.d. Rights in and responsibilities for technical data and computer software under federal awards, Association of University Technology Managers Technology Transfer Manual: Managing the Invention Disclosure, Review and Protection Processes, third ed., vol. 1.

Massey Licata, J., 2009. How to Protect Intellectual Property and Still Publish, Association of University Technology Managers Technology Transfer Manual: Managing the Invention Disclosure, Review and Protection Processes, third ed., vol. 3.

Nelson, L., 2007. Evaluating Inventions from Research Institutions. In: Krattiger, A., Mahoney, R.T., Nelsen, L. (Eds.), Intellectual Property management in Health and Agricultural Innovation: A Handbook of Best practices MIHR, Oxford, UK, and PIPRA: Davis, USA. Available online at: <www.iphandbook.org>.

35 U.S.C. § 154 (2013).

Stewart, P., Jenkins, R., 2009. Managing joint authorship and ownership of copyrighted works, Association of University Technology Managers Technology Transfer Manual: Managing the Invention Disclosure, Review and Protection Processes, third ed., vol. 3.

The University of Kansas, (n.d.) Innovation and Collaboration. Protecting Intellectual Property. Lawrence, KS

White, A.E., 2009. Ownership of University Inventions in the United States. Association of University Technology Managers Technology Transfer Manual: Managing the Invention Disclosure, Review and Protection Processes, third ed., vol. 3.

Further Reading

Di Sante, A.C., 2007. The role of the inventor in the technology transfer process. In: Krattiger, A., Mahoney, R.T., Nelsen, L. (Eds.), Intellectual Property Management in Health and Agricultural Innovation: A Handbook of Best Practices MIHR, Oxford, UK, and PIPRA: Davis, USA. Available online at: <www.ipHandbook.org>.

Chapter 8

Intangible Asset Training

Introduction

This chapter was not designed to describe in comprehensive detail the full content of an intangible asset training program for companies. Should this have been my intent, it would have necessitated articulating a very broad curriculum, with little attention to distinguishing and safeguarding intangibles and each variation relevant to individual industry sectors, which would have been tediously long.

So, as somewhat of an act of operational compromise, I opted to draw the reader's attention to the three most challenging aspects of bringing intangible asset training to companies:

1. *The Why:* Articulating a strong business rationale for why companies should engage in intangible asset training and why it's warranted, justified, and absolutely necessary.
2. *The Who:* For whom, within a company's organizational hierarchy, should intangible asset training be at least initially directed?
3. *The Benefits:* What benefits can a company expect as a result of engaging in intangible asset training?

An unfortunate reality is that intangible assets, conceptually speaking, remain, in many industry sectors and business transaction environments, elusive, overlooked, undervalued, and unprotected. Any one of these missteps or miscues assumes greater significance for companies and their management teams insofar as not having the operational practices in place—that is, the capability to identify and unravel a company's intangible assets; assess their contributory value; and develop, exploit, and convert them to sources of value, revenue, competitive advantage, and the correct safeguards.

This chapter begins with the premise that management teams and boards are obligated to routinely and objectively ask: Is our company properly positioned insofar as possessing the expertise and skill sets to identify, unravel, develop, differentiate, exploit, and extract as much value as possible from our intangible assets, while monitoring and safeguarding the asset's materiality, value, and sources of revenue they create?

As conveyed numerous times throughout this book, albeit in different ways, the embodiment of intangible asset training lies in the capability to design and execute the necessary policies, practices, and procedures to sustain control, use, and ownership, and monitor the value, materiality, and risk to a company's intangible assets.

In today's business and transaction environments, which are competitive, aggressive, globally predatorial, and increasingly dominated by intangible assets, if the preceding does not occur, is poorly executed and administered, or fails, little else may matter, because risks will surely materialize with asset value and materiality quickly diminishing, if not "go to zero."

Define Intangible Assets in Business Contexts

As a longtime intangible asset strategist, a genuinely frustrating aspect to ongoing initiatives to broaden and elevate awareness about intangible assets and how to effectively exploit them is the esoterically unhelpful language frequently used in defining intangibles—that is, they lack physicality, are nonphysical, cannot be seen or touched, have no set monetary value, and their performance and value are challenging to objectively measure.

So, compared to definitions attached to tangible assets with their well-recognized and multiple contributions to the conventional business bottom line, intangible assets in most instances have yet to achieve a comparable level of business clarity. There are exceptions, of course, and they typically lie with companies and management teams whose value and sources of revenue are firmly and irreversibly embedded in knowledge, or the intangible asset-intensive arenas.

I have encountered countless situations in which management teams, boards, investors, and employees alike still struggle to make sense of what the British euphemistically describe as the "invisibles." In part, the British characterization of intangible assets is very understandable because, seldom, if ever, are intangible assets reported on company balance sheets or financial statements.

Still, business leaders today would be hard-pressed to deny the reality that steadily rising numbers of companies have fewer tangible (physical) assets in their inventory. Instead, their physical inventories are being replaced with intangible assets. Because of this, operational familiarity with intangible assets is essential to most companies' near- and long-term success and bottom line, including their viability, sustainability, market space, stability, competitiveness, revenue generation, and value. To those management teams who still express dismissiveness and elect to remain operationally unfamiliar with intangible assets and their contributory role and value, intangible asset training can be challenging insofar as leading them to achieve the much-needed "Ah ha!" moment.

Special Categories of Intangible Assets

There are special categories of intangible assets, a segment of which are knowledge-based collections of intellectual, structural, and relationship capital that originate and are held between our respective ears or stored electronically, issued to our company as intellectual property, particularly patents, or merely the accumulation of experience and specialized know-how that has been optimally linked to help understand how and when to use that know-how effectively and profitably.

Remain within Comfort Zones

Whether a company and its management teams and employees are operating a financially successful intangible asset-intensive business or conducting scientific research, such as an R&D project, a large percentage of management teams appear preferably inclined to remain within their own quantitative comfort zones, which frequently consist of facts, numbers, formulas, and ratios. Under these circumstances, one's comfort zone is fairly easy to sustain because the measurement tools we have grown accustomed to using and relying on for decision making and business analysis are perceived as producing tangible data wherein a high number or high percentage means one thing and a low number or low percentage means something different.

These assumed comfort zones of hard numbers are becoming more obscure as the persistent dominance of intangible assets is factored. In such instances, management teams, boards, and employees alike can be challenged, through well-designed intangible asset training, to push their conventional perspectives beyond the tangible to the intangible relative to the contributory value intangible assets deliver to companies and organizations.

Intangible Asset Training Venues: It's Not Always Easy

As noted previously, intangible assets are not the simplest of subjects to define to business audiences, particularly *those* unfamiliar with, unaccustomed to, or hesitant to recognize *their* contributions to a company's value, sources of revenue, or as underliers to competitive advantages.

Unfortunately, intangible assets are, in many instances, still perceived and interpreted as obscure theoretical concepts best suited for university lecture halls rather than real-world business applications. Anecdotally, I suspect many of the challenges and uneasiness lies in intangible assets lack of physicality and the overall untidiness and subjectivity associated with measuring, managing, reporting, or accounting for intangible assets through most conventional or customary practices or methodologies.

So, those conducting briefings, seminars, and awareness training about these elusive (nonphysical) assets are well advised to have a broad repertoire of examples and practical applications at the ready, to address questions, criticisms, and skepticisms that arise, particularly about strategies for intangible asset exploitation—that is, commercialization, monetization, etc.

Intangible asset training objectives include describing how to collectively demonstrate better, smarter, and more effective techniques to identify, assess, develop, utilize, manage, and exploit a company's intangible assets as integral attributes that can be converted to value, sources of revenue, and competitive advantages.

That is why it's absolutely essential for intangible asset trainers to ensure as much business, economic, and competitive-advantage clarity as possible is conveyed to minimize any continued; hesitancy about intangible assets, and management teams' obligation to aggressively and consistently engage their company's intangible assets now!

Intangible asset training objectives are clear—that is, they describe what intangible assets are, what they aren't, the various forms they take, and strategies in which they can be effectively exploited. Achieving these training objectives will lay necessary foundations to advance most every company's competitiveness, its value, and revenue-generation capabilities.

Training Challenges

UNDERSTANDING THE ABSENCE OF PHYSICALITY

If a tree falls in a forest when no person is around, does it make a sound? Sure it does. But, the noise itself may be irrelevant if no one is present to hear it and no action is necessary. Similarly, if a company's asset that happens to be intangible is stolen, misappropriated, infringed, or pirated by an adversary, will its absence be noticed? The reality is it may not, unless there is an active asset monitoring process in place.

One thing that is needed for sure is a clear, concise, and sector-relevant definition of intangible assets that is operational in character and is absent a dominant accounting, legal, and regulatory orientation.

MAKING DEFINITIONS OF INTANGIBLE ASSETS OPERATIONAL

While attending a conference at the National Academies several years ago titled "Intangible Assets: Measuring and Enhancing Their Contribution to Corporate Value and Economic Growth," one speaker euphemistically and with a condescending tone characterized the difference between *tangible* and *intangible* assets in the following manner: "If you can kick it, drop it, or stub your toe on it, it's a tangible asset." Presumably, if one can do neither, it's an intangible asset. That is hardly the kind of definition that exudes confidence among management teams about the utilization and exploitation of intangible assets.

Today, regardless of what products, services, or systems a company produces or, whether it's a large multinational or a small- to medium-size enterprise, it's increasingly likely that valuable (proprietary) intellectual, structural, and relationship capital are thoroughly embedded in a company's products and services.

What is often missing in these definitions though, to benefit business decision makers, management teams, and boards, is:

- A clearer recognition for the forms intangible asset-generated value takes, and recognizing the various formats intangible assets exist in in conjunction with assessing their respective contributory value.
- The practicalities and strategies for extracting value from intangible assets.
- Determining best practices to sustain control, use, and ownership, and monitor value, materiality, and risks to intangible assets throughout their respective value.

Recognizing and respecting the reality that ideas and innovation in the form of intellectual, relationship, and structural capital, that are regularly produced internally, are routinely and unceremoniously embedded in a company's products and services while fully appreciating their linkage to other intangible assets, such as reputation, brand, goodwill, and competitive advantages, is important to the sustainability of any company.

Ideas Are Intangible Assets

Jack Welch, former chairman of General Electric, made numerous contributions and left a substantial legacy relative to the way large corporations are structured, and ultimately managed. Many of those legacies are still attempted today, one in particular, whereby he was purported to quickly recognize the key elements of a given issue or challenge and then set about separating and distilling the proverbial "fluff" to arrive at a generally profitable way forward.

Two examples are conveyed here through statements attributed to Welch:

1. An idea is not necessarily a biotech idea ... that is the wrong view of what an idea is.... An idea is an error-free billing system ... an idea is taking a process that used to require six days to do and getting it done in one day ... we get 6 to 7 percent productivity increases routinely now, mostly because of ideas like that ... everyone can contribute (Welch, 2008).
2. An organization's ability to learn and translate learning into action rapidly, is the ultimate competitive advantage (Welch, 2014).

A business impetus for developing and executing on ideas internally generated are that they can manifest as intellectual and structural capital that company management teams are obliged, more so than ever before, to recognize the importance of having processes in place whereby relevant ideas can be safely articulated, assessed, and, accordingly, rise to the surface. That requires effective training that, among other things, draws attention to the role of intangible assets.

But, crossing the intangible asset chasm through training is often threatened by obstacle courses of skepticism, organizational bureaucracy, and the inevitable and proverbial "This is the way it's always been done, why change it now?" This frequently translates as:

- A reluctance to acknowledge the intangible assets a firm produces and possesses.
- An absence of personal and managerial confidence in ways to improve the positioning, utilization, exploitation, and extraction of value from a company's intangible assets.
- Unfounded concerns or misconceptions about the resources, costs, time, and processes necessary to elevate intangible assets as routine action items on corporate agendas.
- Professional (personal) embarrassment about having not already taken the necessary affirmative action to address the above.

One would think, given the economic fact that rising percentages of most company's value, sources of revenue, and competitive advantage emanate directly from intangible assets, that it shouldn't be that difficult to cast such skepticisms and reluctance aside to receive the message that a company's intangible assets absolutely must be on discussion agendas in board rooms globally.

Intangible Asset Training to Exploit Risk Taking

There is no shortage of evidence to indicate significant percentages of business leaders are, by their nature, and on various levels, risk takers. That is, there is little or no aversion to engage in ventures or activities that carry known levels of risk. With respect to intangible asset training then, it's somewhat perplexing why business leaders and management team members generally remain unready to fully and aggressively engage their intangible assets, but instead continue down their respective path of conventional past practices.

Intangible Asset Training Is Not Merely Theoretical

A particularly stimulating conversation occurred recently with a very astute colleague. The colleague certainly intended no disrespect to me by suggesting that the development, use, and exploitation of intangible assets remains largely theoretical. Without elaboration, I presumed she meant intangible assets, in general, lacked sufficiently practical, bottom-line (business) relevance to move outside the theoretical realm, a position of which I obviously disagree!

Having taught in universities for 25+ years, I can say, without hesitation, that a significant percentage of the time when I uttered the word "theory" in a classroom or at a professional conference, the initial reaction was similar in both instances. That is, with a fair amount of consistency, the following tended to occur in sequence: a muffled, but audible sigh, followed by a glazing of the eyes, as if to say, we're going to take a nap now while this guy (me) tries to explain a theory that we're already inclined to presume has little, if any, relevance to our real business world.

Unfortunately, there remain some audiences who remain inclined to crudely characterize theories as merely constituting one's guess, hunch, or untested opinion derived exclusively from a book and not the real business world.

To seasoned intangible asset trainers and strategists, it's frustrating and unfortunate to hear otherwise intelligent, experienced, savvy, and successful business persons convey dismissiveness, or worse, reject well-established and globally recognized economic facts about intangible assets by characterizing them as unsubstantiated (theories) that will not hold up to the global scrutiny, rigors, and stresses of today's aggressive and competitive business (transaction) environments.

The Brookings Institute, Athena Alliance, IC Knowledge Center, the Intangible Asset Finance Society, and other prominent "think tanks" and professional associations comprised largely of senior practitioners were, after all, influenced to engage intangible assets and become subject-matter experts due to intangible assets' conspicuous role in all business transactions; the need for effective stewardship, oversight, management, exploitation, and monetization of intangible assets; and the reality that conventional financial statements and balance sheets do not convey a complete picture of a company's real financial health absent factoring the role and contributory value of intangible assets.

Training Designed to Develop Internal Intangible Asset Strategists

It's not merely a cliché, nor is it unsubstantiated marketing to recognize the economic fact that 80+% of most company's value, sources of revenue, and building blocks for growth, profitability, and sustainability lie in or evolve directly from intangible assets. This is a globally universal business and economic reality. Respectfully, reluctance to engage this economic fact is misguided and certainly contributes to companies and their management teams remaining behind the business transaction, competitive advantage, and value curve and not rising to their potential.

In today's tightly wound, highly compressed, and increasingly and globally aggressive and predatorial business transaction environment, management teams that routinely hand-off intangible asset issues, to be disposed of by legal counsel or accounting units, are assuming intangible assets are legal and accounting versus business management and decision issues. To those, I respectfully encourage them to read further!

Training Outcomes

Intangible asset training should deliver strategies for the following advanced outcomes:

1. Provide ongoing best-practice guidance to companies, an important aspect of which is to ensure intangible assets are effectively safeguarded, monitored, and exploited.
2. Add predictability to business transaction outcomes (i.e., projected returns) and exit strategies by addressing asset stability, fragility, defensibility, and value sustainability in both pre- and post-transaction contexts.
3. How to conduct intangible asset assessments and due diligence to identify, unravel, safeguard, and monitor intangible assets to create synergies, efficiencies, value, new sources of revenue and competitive advantages, etc.
4. Reduce the probability that a project's or transaction's momentum will be stifled by recognizing, assessing, and mitigating circumstances, which can entangle

intangible assets in costly and time-consuming legal challenges or disputes; undermine asset value and performance; and adversely affect (company) reputation risk points (e.g., regulatory compliance, product/service quality, security breaches).

5. Introduce company-centric knowledge management and balanced scorecard initiatives to facilitate creation of an intangible asset-intelligent company culture that is aligned with a company's mission, business objectives, and new initiatives.

6. Design comprehensive organizational resilience plans that specifically encompass mission-essential intangible assets—that is, those that create value, sources of revenue, and company/sector competitive advantages to provide quicker recovery following the materialization of a substantial risk or significant business disruption or disaster. Too, because of the persistent, global, and asymmetric risks and threats to intangible assets, it's instructive to recognize that growing percentages of risks to company's intangible assets have become inevitabilities when they are left unrecognized and unmanaged.

Stone v. Ritter Has Made Operational Familiarity with Intangible Assets A Fiduciary Responsibility

As referenced in Reese and Compton (2007), the Delaware court decision in *Stone v. Ritter* (911 A.2d 362) (Del. 2006) drew much warranted attention to the necessity to consistently provide practical context to company boards, as fiduciary responsibilities, regarding a company's assets, with specific implication to intangible assets.

This court decision brings clarity to the obligations of boards to be kept apprised of what is going on inside their company as good-faith duties or duties of loyalty; to ensure the company has sufficient (asset) monitoring and reporting (compliance) systems in place to routinely and properly keep them apprised; and to allow them (within their respective scope) to reach informed judgments concerning a company's compliance with law and business performance.

In other words, each is obliged to assume a more hands-on position with respect to the stewardship, oversight, and management of, among other things, their company's intangible assets.

The relevance of *Stone v. Ritter* lies in the fact that important information failed to reach board members due to what the court determined to be ineffective internal company controls, processes, and regular monitoring of those controls. So, for those who may not find these decisions particularly relevant, one need not look further than the veritable parade of senior corporate executives and government agency heads testifying before Congress about errors and omissions in judgment and action—that is, what did you know, when did you know it, and what did you do about it after you became aware of it?

Intangible Asset Training Is Not An Impediment to Company Productivity

True, some decision makers and management teams will regard the presence of intangible asset training as being unnecessary or possibly even an impediment or hindrance to their *go fast, go hard, go global* agendas.

Those management teams who elect to continue conveying a sense of dismissiveness toward intangible assets by, for example, indefinitely putting off any intangible asset training and implementing actions stemming from such training will be doing so at their company's financial and reputational peril.

So, when the proposition of having intangible asset operational familiarity training is framed in this context, management teams could quite correctly conclude it would be prudent to seek and demand answers, as a fiduciary responsibility, to this question: Is this company effectively positioned insofar as possessing the tactical and strategic expertise necessary to produce the requisite information to keep senior management consistently and sufficiently informed about the status of and how best to utilize, manage, and safeguard their company's intangible assets?

As more management teams and boards reflect on and ultimately come to recognize how much of their company's value and sources of revenue are dependent on consistent production, effective development, use, management, and safeguarding of their intangible assets, training is more likely to resonate and manifest as an irrefutable rationale for dedicating time, resources, and personnel to ensure the highest echelons of company decision, strategy, and policy making are kept duly apprised.

Global Paradigm Shift

Beginning in the late 1990s and early 2000s with the publication of The Brookings Institutes' "Intangibles Project Report" coupled with New York University's Stearn School of Business and Dr. Baruch Lev's creation of the Intangible Asset Research Center, important and game-changing groundwork was being laid for recognizing that a global paradigm shift had indeed occurred. The shift itself was quite straightforward: intangible assets had become the overwhelmingly dominant source of most company's value, sources of revenue, profitability, sustainability, and competitive advantage globally.

What precipitated this global paradigm shift was the reality that a substantial percentage of businesses and companies had, or indeed were in the midst of, transitioning to the knowledge era. This means rising percentages of global economies, as a whole, were being both stimulated and dominated by the production, utilization, and exploitation of intangible assets in the form of intellectual, structural, and relationship capital; brand; and reputation.

Collectively, this led to a new species of business: those that are intangible asset intensive and intangible asset driven.

Key Objective to Intangible Asset Training for Management Teams

In many instances, intangible assets, particularly intellectual, structural, and relationship capital, can emerge, mature, and become integrated in various aspects of a company's operations and processes. But, they often do so under the radar—that is, without recognition, safeguards, or monitoring. When this occurs, the probability that all or a portion of those assets will become vulnerable to compromise, misappropriation, or infringement, or merely meld into the public domain is predictably high.

Once such risks materialize, recovering the assets' full contributory value, uncontested use, and competitive advantages they previously delivered will very likely be a costly and time-consuming undertaking with a low probability of achieving either rapid or comprehensive success. Also, a frequently exacerbating aspect to public awareness of the event is to elevate a company's vulnerability to the materialization of additional reputation (image, goodwill) risks.

In other words, achieving a completely favorable outcome—that is, all assets being returned with their value, revenue-generating capabilities, and competitive advantages intact—is low. This is why organizational resilience should be fully integrated in intangible asset training. When risks or threats to a company's intangible assets materialize, having personnel with operational familiarity of these assets can go a long way toward mitigating the impact. That is, an effective and tested organizational resilience plan should render a company capable of maintaining or rapidly returning to a state of relative operational normalcy during or immediately following a potentially devastating calamity. For example, as Hurricane Katrina was ravaging the Gulf Coasts of Florida, Alabama, Mississippi, and the entire city of New Orleans, the devastation was significant and long term. Yes, this was an especially horrific storm, but few businesses had resilience plans sufficient to accommodate natural disasters of this magnitude other than to temporarily close for extended periods of time or permanently relocate, which we know many elected to do.

Several years ago, I was engaged to develop a comprehensive organizational resilience plan for a large multinational firm. The nature of this firm's business was such that it was dependent on local, state, and federal government entities to achieve a state of resilience should a natural disaster risk materialize. After investigating and deliberating some time on this issue, I submitted a detailed report that strongly advised the company to consider three options:

1. To immediately allocate sufficient resources internally to have at the ready qualified personnel, materials, and equipment necessary to return key (certainly not all) functionality to an operational state in 48–72 hours following the event, which is exceptionally generous.
2. Focus on shifting operations to other company sites.
3. Garner sufficient political support (local, state, and federal) to give this firm regulatory priority insofar as aid needed to return the firm to even partial operational normalcy.

Reputation Risk Influences Management Teams to be More Receptive to Intangible Asset Training

Influencing management teams to recognize the necessity to seek and secure intangible asset training should be a relatively straightforward and not a particularly complicated decision. Unfortunately, but quite realistically, motivation to seek intangible asset training is often influenced by the growing number of highly publicized adverse events, acts, missteps, and miscues that manifest as reputational risks with some regularity; consider GM, Toyota, BP, Pharma, etc.

A company's reputation, remember, is one category of intangible asset. As such, materialized risk to a company's reputation warrants time for a management team to figure out how the same or similar event could rematerialize to adversely affect reputation, and in some instances put the continued existence of the company itself at risk. This is another aspect to effective intangible asset training.

With respect to mitigating company reputation risks, the following are factors that should favorably influence management teams to seek intangible asset training:

- Heightened recognition for the globally asymmetric risks and threats that rapidly materialize with particular adverse impact to reputation, brand, and asset value.
- Accelerated innovation and product development times, and abbreviated asset functionality cycles and product launch windows, all of which are increasingly dependent on intangible assets and effect on reputation.
- The geographically boundaryless speed that intangible assets originate and mature and contribute to a company's reputation.
- Increasing global universality of intangible assets and regulatory attention, particularly reporting their value, performance, materiality, and reputation.

It Is Important That Intangible Asset Training Includes Company's Higher Echelons

Admittedly, intangible asset training for management teams is somewhat new. After all, The Brookings Institute's initial report on intangible assets, along with numerous papers, articles, and books that spun off from that initiative, articulate the relevance of intangible assets, but do not enjoy the wide circulation they warrant.

Some would argue that engaging higher company echelons in intangible asset training is not the place to start. The rationale is that frequently higher managerial echelons are too busy and time constrained so they are less likely to adjust intellectually or operationally to fully appreciate the relevance of intangible assets and the necessity to strategize how to effectively exploit them.

Obviously, I hold the view that intangible asset awareness and operational familiarity training must commence at not just the highest echelons, but also on the shop floor, if for no other reason than to dramatize intangible assets as sources value, revenue, and competitive advantage, and recognize intangible asset originators and contributors.

To demonstrate this, several years ago I conducted an internal intangible asset assessment for a midsize firm with multiple domestic and international manufacturing and sales sites associated with their global product. What my assessment revealed was that lower-echelon employees were, in a large percentage of instances, the actual originators and developers of their company's usually strong array of intangible assets, but seldom, if ever, were acknowledged for those strategic, value, and competitive-advantage assets.

Challenges Remain to Intangible Asset Training Receptivity

One of the single biggest challenges to companies being receptive to intangible asset training is, in my judgment, that financial statements and balance sheets still constitute reliable guides for determining a company's standing. However, seldom, if ever, do these documents account for intangible assets other than generically lumping them together as goodwill. Nor do they provide management teams with a strategically dynamic portrait of a company's actual status—that is, its fiscal and competitive-advantage health and soundness.

Conventional financial statements and balance sheets do describe whether or not financial targets are being achieved. In fairness, neither were designed to capture a company's qualitative vital signs, or serve as the sole source on which business decisions were to be made. So, in that context, these conventional instruments remain relevant for business accounting, auditing, and analysis rooted in tax and accounting law and associated regulatory mandates.

Still, astute financial analysts and intangible asset strategists can, together with a company's financial statement and balance sheet, collectively make better business decisions because the art and science of the intangible asset side of the business are factored in. Continued reliance on these conventional practices, absent inclusion of intangible assets, is akin to operating an airplane with its radar and air-to-ground communication system functioning haphazardly, which obviously triggers skepticism among passengers and flight crew as to the flight's outcome.

Therefore, training personnel to track and monitor the performance of a company's intangible assets is not a time-resource luxury applicable only to large, fortune-ranked companies; rather, it's a training necessity and fiduciary imperative for all companies.

Operational Familiarity of Intangible Assets Produces Multipliers

Valuable and immediately useful multipliers accrue from a well-designed and executed intangible asset awareness training program, including:

- Reducing uncertainty and adding predictability to intangible asset-dominated operations and transactions by addressing the importance of consistent monitoring of their value, stability, fragility, and defensibility, relative to achieving projected returns, competitive-market/sector positioning, and creating structural synergies and efficiencies.
- Identifying new market-entry opportunities by distinguishing and integrating relevant intellectual, structural, and relationship capital.
- Reducing the probability that intangible assets will become entangled in costly, time-consuming, and momentum-stifling legal challenges that impede project and company growth, and undermine asset value, competitiveness, and performance.
- Recognizing that patents alone are no longer stand-alone or reliable indicators of company value and transaction predictability, nor do they serve as an effective deterrent to infringement or misappropriation.
- Forging stronger relationships with legal counsel, auditors, and accountants on matters related to intangible assets.
- Aligning a company's business practices and external business transactions with risk assessment, asset management, due diligence, and strategies to sustain and enhance asset value.

- Elevating awareness, alertness, and accountability for identifying and communicating significant risks, threats, and challenges (related to intangible assets, IP, and proprietary competitive advantages) in business transactions before irreversible economic hemorrhaging occurs.
- Elevating a company's stature and goodwill among its customers, suppliers, and investors, and gain attention of audiences beyond a company's traditional markets.
- Identifying techniques for structuring business operations to sustain the contracted levels of control, use, ownership, value, and brand integrity of the assets, and mitigate the undermining of projected competitive advantages.

Each of these multipliers represent examples of how an activity, such as intangible asset awareness training can produce positive affects that can reverberate throughout a company to breed even greater and more sustainable outcomes.

References

Welch, J., 2008. Guide to Management Ideas and Gurus' The Economist, With Tim Handle. Profile Books Ltd., p. 9.

Welch, J., 2014. <http://www.brainyquote.com/quotes/quotes/j/jackwelch173305.html>.

Reese, C., Compton, K., 2007. Directors Beware: Ignorance can mean big bucks, not bliss. Technology Times, Tech Law, p. 6.

Chapter 9

Measuring Performance of Intangible Assets

Operational Familiarity with Intangible Assets

This chapter is about the persistent challenge that intangible asset strategists routinely experience in regards to influencing management teams and investors to take relatively nonintrusive and inexpensive steps to improve the financial and competitive health of their companies. Largely, that challenge evolves around the importance of putting in place consistent and straightforward practices that provide for the stewardship, oversight, and management of a company's intangible assets.

In this regard, Deloitte (2004, 2007) produced two relevant and insightful reports that expressed the view that conventional financial statements/balance sheets do not robotically provide a complete or comprehensive picture of any company's "soundness." A long-held conviction that conventional financial statements and balance sheets are the only or absolute best instrument for conveying a company's soundness, should, in 2014 and beyond, not be taken for granted.

There's little doubt that continued reliance on conventional business accounting practices, coupled with institutional resistance to change, collectively influences management teams to remain reluctant to engage their intangible assets in a more aggressive and consistent manner, and, in some instances, be utterly dismissive to the potentially lucrative outcomes embedded in their company's intangible assets.

Of course, conventional financial statements that place emphasis on identifying whether or not financial targets have been achieved remain necessary, and are not something that I'm advocating doing away with. Rather, I'm merely encouraging management teams to seek operational familiarity with their intangible assets on par with their familiarity with conventional practices.

Why Is More Balance Necessary?

The key reason, as cited in Deloitte's reports (2004, 2007), is that conventional financial measures are simply not designed to capture the many necessary qualitative aspects that we now know are unequivocally and directly related to business success, particularly those found in a company's intangible assets. For example, these reports cannot outline the financial rewards of building and strengthening a company's relationship capital with its various stakeholders and other constituency groups up and down its respective value-supply chain.

Fortunately there are several factors today at work to influence management teams to pay more attention to observing, engaging, and monitoring their key intangible assets, including:

- Increasing global competition, irrespective of company size, sector, maturity, or product/service. This includes acknowledging the importance and influence of human capital—intellectual, structural, and relationship—dispersed throughout a company's value-supply chain, and the boundary-less speed in which that capital can be acquired and disseminated globally.
- The growing significance of building and sustaining relationship capital with customers and clients. This includes a heightened awareness by management teams of the foundational value of a company's reputation, and the increasing frequency of instantaneous, long-lasting, and sometimes irreversible cascading effects that can occur when reputation risks materialize. Also, there is greater global scrutiny by various media forums and outlets on issues other than solely a company's financial performance.
- The accelerating product innovation and launch times before competitive-advantage erosion can occur.
- The increasing country-specific regulatory attention to reporting and measuring intangible assets.

Obviously, it would be desirable if management teams, boards, and investors begin to regard the oversight, stewardship, and management of intangible asset metrics not merely as some unnecessary or altruistic task, but rather as an important and prudent business practice integral to sustaining and enhancing every company's value, revenue, profitability, and competitive advantages.

Example: Measuring the Intangible Assets Delivered by IT Security

As Charles Kettering (n.d.) put it, "a problem well stated is a problem half solved." That is surely the case for information technology (IT) security in companies. Some things like IT security may appear, at least on the surface, easily measurable. This is because, in large part, various information technologies are so ubiquitous that management teams, regardless of whether their firm has information security officers employed, assume they understand the rudiments of IT security, and, therefore, what the performance measurement points are.

Being a security practitioner for over 25 years, I recognize that security remains somewhat vague and ambiguous, even in 2014; that is, until management teams can precisely describe, at the outset, their performance expectation following deployment of security services and products. Presumably, performance expectations would be measurable reductions in risk, coupled with less uncertainty about outcomes for particular IT-dependent projects and transactions.

On the other hand, security, in the sense of a personal feeling of being more safe and secure, can mean different things to different people, sometimes dependent on time, location, circumstance, or venue. But, an often agreed-on perspective about security is, once security is in place, there will be some corresponding and favorable change in risk and uncertainty. As Hubbard (2010) points to many times in his book, if someone is fuzzy about what he or she expects to observe as an outcome of a security system or service, it's likely any subsequent quantitative and qualitative performance measurements will be equally fuzzy.

Thus, for starters, it can be very useful for a company if definitional consensus is reached regarding the terms *risk* and *uncertainty* to avoid misunderstandings in subsequent performance assessments. *Uncertainty* is merely the lack of having complete certainty about, for example, business decisions. In other words, a particular business decision may have multiple possibilities that exist with the actual outcome remaining unknown (uncertain) because other possibilities exist or variables come into play. *Risk*, on the other hand, includes a specific and broader state of uncertainty in which multiple possibilities exist, and, should they materialize, will result in some type or degree of loss or other undesirable outcome to a company's assets.

Measuring uncertainty then for IT security is measuring a particular set of probabilities that a chief security officer (CSO), chief technology officer (CTO), chief information officer (CIO), and chief information security officer (CISO) has set. For example, following deployment of a correct IT security product or system, a company may project a 60% reduction in the probability that proprietary data or information would be subject of illegal extraction. Actual measurement of risk would include identifying a fairly comprehensive list of inadvertent or intentional adverse events and acts.

Measuring the Correct Intangible Asset Value Streams

While the conventional view of financial statements being the sole measurement of a company's performance is understandable, I have yet to engage any companies that were alike regarding how their intangible assets were being acknowledged or utilized. That is, most companies have company- and project-specific blends of intangible assets being utilized.

Supportive of this perspective is a 2001 study produced by U.K.'s Department of Trade and Industry (DTI) Future and Innovation Unit that revealed seven specific intangible asset value streams that form the foundation for unlocking a company's true potential. The findings of the study evolved from in-depth interviews with 50 successful organizations to identify "the intangible raw materials that employees use to ... collaborate with one another, in order to achieve company goals, solve company problems, and exploit opportunities for profitability and growth."

The seven intangible value streams identified in the DTI study are the following:

1. Building an effective strategy for managing and maintaining relationships with key stakeholders that entails understanding how to identify key (internal and external) stakeholders and develop, organize, and sustain that network of relationships; and recognizing that the nexus of ideas and opportunities evolving from that network will play an important role toward achieving and sustaining a company's competitive advantage. The added value a company can achieve from the effective management and use of its largely internally held intellectual and structural capital and company-/project-specific expertise. In the globally competitive business transaction environment, a company's survival is interwoven with management teams' ability to ensure the knowledge and expertise developed internally and acquired externally are effectively and consistently shared and used throughout an enterprise, particularly the tacit knowledge and expertise that's held in the minds of individual employees.

2. Absent a system for knowledge and expertise dissemination and sharing within a company, any company will be less likely to identify gaps in their knowledge/expertise base; respond quickly enough to identify, assess, and act on potential opportunities; and will become more vulnerable to unexpected losses of

knowledge/expertise, such as a key employee leaving or the misappropriation of high proprietary information.

3. Communicating clarity of purpose to employees' role in recognizing and understanding the importance of achieving a balance between achieving company goals, and the daily operational need for building and sustaining intangible asset value through their intellectual, structural, and relationship capital.

4. Building a sustainable and flexible company culture that encourages greater awareness of new and changing market developments, and facilitates a quicker grasp of and produces a more timely and effective response to exploiting any new developments and opportunities.

5. Regardless of the quality of the product or service a company produces, it's likely neither will add value to the company if their reputation with consumers, customers, clients, and suppliers is poor, has been damaged, or is otherwise impaired. A company's reputation, expectations, and trust have become the foundations for building and sustaining competitive advantages and market position. Company management teams and boards who give little credence to those objective and essential components to success will likely be similarly dismissive about the rapidity that risks to a company's reputation can emerge and materialize to create irrevocable damage and losses.

6. Maintaining the correct mix of employee competency—that is, skills, knowledge, and expertise—are important enablers of growth in both capacity and scope. This requires management team commitment to consistent investments in developing and maintaining employee talents, which are essential to not merely support existing operations, processes, and programs, but also as effective contributors to future company initiatives and strategic planning.

7. Maintaining market position and competitive advantages today involves, among other things, ensuring that management teams and boards have the right processes and systems in place, at the right time, and at the right location to support company activities and initiatives as needed. However, in today's seemingly nanosecond timeframes when markets, transactions, and the needs and demands of stakeholders can change and risks rapidly materialize, those company processes and systems must be sufficiently flexible and adaptable to accommodate those changes and execute at an equally rapid pace.

Financial reporting systems focus on historic balance sheets, profits, and cash flow, but management teams and boards don't necessarily get the right perception of assets' prospective value through such a historical lens only. Value is an uncertain and increasingly risk-laden factor embedded in the global business environment with success being dependent on objective assessments being conducted that address future options and opportunities and extrapolations of historic costs as well as current asset performance.

Creating Value from Intangible Assets

At the nexus of the knowledge-based economy lie three variously interwoven factors: global competitiveness, continually changing technologies, and the ability to create, sustain, and extract value from intangible assets. The latter factor is becoming an increasingly relevant metric for assessing management team effectiveness on two levels:

- Recognizing and grasping future opportunities will depend on identifying, managing, and developing a company's full spectrum of intangible assets.
- Consistency of company preparedness to engage and correctly execute initiatives focused on building and extracting value from intangible assets.

A useful starting point for achieving this worthy and necessary strategy is through the inclusion of the seven key intangible asset streams noted earlier in the chapter. Collectively, these intangible assets form the essential ingredients upon which a company's future success can be built. In short:

- Relationships
- Tacit knowledge
- Leadership and communication
- Company culture
- Reputation and trust
- Skills and competencies
- Processes and systems

The report characterizes these as ingredients to the intangible raw materials that talented employees use to engage with one another to achieve goals, solve problems, identify opportunities, and maximize their potential. To achieve the returns that these assets are potentially capable of, management teams and boards should invest in them, do what's necessary to sustain them, and genuinely manage them as the strategic assets they are.

Measuring Performance and Value of Intangible Assets

Effective and consistent utilization and management of a company's intangible assets is one of the most important and significant interventions a management team can undertake. This is *not* merely overdramatized conjecture; rather it's a business reality *and* fiduciary responsibility that will deliver returns.

The intangible value of a company is, put quite simply, the difference between its market value (share price multiplied by the number of shares issued) and its net book value (recorded value of all tangible assets). So, if a company's intangible assets were valued at 100 million U.S. dollars, even a 1% loss in value would be significant, whereas a 1% gain would translate as substantial shareholder profits.

For most companies today, seldom does their intangible asset value fall below 50% of the market value. Clearly, the more knowledge, know-how, branding, reputation, competitive-advantage intensive a company is, the higher its intangible value is, which routinely ranges from 65% to as high as 90%.

However, when a company's most valuable intangible assets are overlooked, dismissed, or neglected, the contributions and competitive advantages those assets deliver frequently become diluted, meld away, or are unwittingly relinquished to competitors that are likely to know how to use them and will do so without hesitation.

References

Deloitt, 2004. In the dark: what boards and executives don't know about the health of their business. Economist. A Survey by Deloitte in Cooperation with the Economist Intelligence Unit.

Deloitt, 2007. In the dark: what many boards and executives still don't know about the health of their business. Economist. A Survey by Deloitte in Cooperation with the Economist Intelligence Unit.

Hubbard, D.W., 2010. How to Measure Anything: Finding the Value of Intangibles in Business, second ed. John Wiley & Sons, Hoboken, NJ.

Charles Kettering. (n.d.). BrainyQuote.com. Retrieved May 9, 2014, from BrainyQuote.com Website: <http://www.brainyquote.com/quotes/quotes/c/charlesket181210.html>

U.K. Department of Trade and Industry, Future and Innovation Unit, 2001. Creating value from your intangible assets: unlocking your true potential. Department of Trade and Industry, UK.

Insider Risks and Threats to Intangible Assets

Chapter 10

The 20-60-20 Rule

Among information asset protection professionals, there is a "rule of thumb" that retains its relevancy since I initially became familiar with it over 25 years ago. It's referred to as the 20-60-20 rule, and many believe it's a reasonable and prudent characterization of today's persistent, annoying, and often successful and costly insider threat.

The rule states that 20% of the people we work with are inherently honest and possess consistently high levels of personal and professional integrity. It's improbable these employees would be intentionally inclined or receptive to engaging in risky, unethical, or dishonest behaviors, acts, or violations of company policies or practices.

Another 20% of the people we work with reside on the opposite end of the spectrum. For these employees, if one were to scratch their thin social-psychological veneer, it's likely what would be found is an inherently dishonest and unethical individual who possesses little, if any, sense of professional and personal integrity

133

or loyalty with respect to consistently complying with company policies or government laws and regulations related to safeguarding intangible assets. This individual, for example, would be receptive to and possess the propensity, when certain opportunities or influencers are presented, to engage in risky, unethical, or illegal acts, such as theft or compromise of valuable and mission-critical information. A particularly disturbing variable to this segment of employees is the increasing number of instances in which individuals are self-motivated to become initiators by engaging in external solicitation initiatives to sell or distribute any information assets they have misappropriated or stolen from their employer. This means they may contact competitors or other economic adversaries to leak or offer for sale their employer's proprietary intangible assets for personal profit or various other reasons.

Then there is the 60% of employees who essentially lie in the middle of this spectrum. These employees typically do not overtly demonstrate any particular receptivity or proclivity to engage in any dishonest, unethical, or illegal acts or behaviors that would purposefully put their employer's intangible assets at risk. However, the outer fringes of this segment, closest to the 20% just characterized, are observant. That is, their future actions and behaviors may be dependent on or influenced by their interpretation of their employers' reactions to or sanctions imposed on fellow employees who are caught violating company information policies.

There is nothing particularly scientific about the 20-60-20 perspective, however the percentages do draw our attention to the persistent challenges presented by "insiders."

Esther Dyson (1995) offered one approach to addressing the insider challenge when she remarked "the trick is to not control the copies of your work, but instead (control) a relationship with the customers-subscriptions, or membership" who can access the proprietary information and intangible assets we endeavor to safeguard. There is certainly a degree of reality to Dyson's remark, at least in terms of assessing employees' propensity, proclivity, or receptivity, at some point in their career, to engage in acts that result in the theft, compromise, misappropriation, or infringement of proprietary intangible assets.

While most of my familiarity with insiders is a direct result of personal experience, I attribute much of my current thinking and approaches for addressing this extraordinary challenge in this chapter to the research by the U.S. DoD's Personnel Security Research Center (PERSEREC) and Carnegie Mellon University's Insider Threat Research Center.

Implications of Insider Research

This section is a summary from a study conducted by PERSEREC (Kramer et al., 2005, 2007). For readers unfamiliar with PERSEREC, it is a relatively small, nondescript arm of the U.S. Department of Defense (DoD) headquartered in Monterrey, CA, that houses an extraordinary group of highly focused researchers committed to conducting a broad range of collaborative research on matters specifically related to personnel security. The product of their research is primarily directed to DoD and various entities within the U.S. intelligence community.

The PERSEREC study analyzed:

- Technological, social, and economic trends that elevate opportunity and motivation for insiders to engage in theft (selling) of classified and proprietary information, and the transfer of materials to foreign rather than domestic recipients.
- Situational factors that affect the frequency that insider espionage, spying, and information theft will occur, rather than analyzing psychological factors that influence a perpetrator's decision.

The study identified the following challenges related to mitigating insider risks and threats:

1. The Internet creates a large and efficient global marketplace for bringing sellers, seekers, brokers, and buyers of information assets together in relative anonymity.
2. Insiders/employees awareness of the value of proprietary information assets that can be sold for a profit.
3. Fewer employees are deterred by a traditional sense of employer loyalty. There is more inclination to view theft of information assets (espionage) to be morally justifiable if sharing those assets will benefit the world community or prevent armed conflict.
4. Internationalization of science and commerce is placing more employees in positions to initiate and maintain contact with international parties, some of whom want to exploit that knowledge that provides seekers, buyers, and brokers of information assets greater opportunity to target, contact, assess, and recruit key developers of protected and proprietary information.
5. Greater inclination for employees engaged in multinational trade transactions to regard unauthorized transfer of information assets or technology as a business matter rather than an act of betrayal or treason.
6. Growing allegiance to a global community—that is, an increasing acceptance of global as well as national values and a tendency to view human society as an evolving system of ethnically and ideologically diverse and interdependent people, thus making illicit acts easier to rationalize.
7. Growing numbers of employees have emotional, ethnic, and financial ties to other countries.
8. Opportunity and motivation factors are converging with vulnerabilities created by one trend being magnified by the negative effects of other trends. There is

no single countervailing trend found on the horizon to make the potential for insider espionage more difficult or less likely to occur.

9. Greater frequency of employees experiencing financial stress from compulsive gambling or other addictions, which provides motivation for selling information for personal gain.

Employee Allegiance: More Challenges to Safeguarding Intangible Assets

This section is directed to management teams, security professionals, legal counsel, HR, and risk managers who are receptive to examining research that has a real and forward-looking bearing on mitigating the rising threats posed by insiders to companies, organizations, and institutions.

In another report produced by PERSEREC (2008), author and principle investigator Katherine Herbig provides readers with much needed insights, perspectives, and facts regarding the single concept of allegiance. Herbig suggests in her report, "Given the current context of globalization, questions about how to assess, investigate, and adjudicate allegiance are of increasing concern." While Herbig correctly notes these concerns are of relevance to the personnel security community and counterintelligence agencies, I might also add these same concerns also have relevance to the private sector, particularly for safeguarding and preserving proprietary intangible assets.

Herbig also points out that "since 1990, more countries are offering dual citizenship to those who immigrate and naturalize elsewhere, but trying to bind those citizens to the countries of origin." Such practices serve, according to Herbig, "to dilute the meaning of citizenship and allegiance."

With respect to this trend, it's not particularly difficult to project that even more complex challenges lie ahead in terms of companies being able to consistently and effectively safeguard their intangible assets in various types of global business transactions. This takes on even greater significance when considered in light of the economic fact that more than 80% of most companies' value and sources of revenue directly evolve from intangible assets and IP, *not* tangible (physical) assets.

The New Insider Threat

With increasing percentages of companies' value and revenue evolving from intangible assets, the new breed of insider threat that has emerged is more calculating and stealthy. These acts can potentially cause more irreversible and immediate harm to a company financially and competitively compared to their predecessors who focused on theft or obtaining an operational familiarity with a company's physical assets.

This is not necessarily about the insider threat posed by the Wen Ho Lee (The Economic Espionage Act of 1996, (USC 1831, 1832)) types of incidents in which classified materials belonging to a national laboratory are compromised and given to an adversary. This chapter is primarily directed to the millions of companies of all sizes that have developed unique sets of intangible assets that deliver their company's value, revenue, and competitive advantages.

When a company does experience theft, misappropriation, or compromise of one or more of its valuable intangible assets by an insider, while the consequences may not be equivalent to broad national security breaches (e.g., WikiLeaks or Edward Snowden's public revelations), the impact to a single company in terms of lost revenue, undermining of competitive advantages, adverse fluctuations in market position, and compromises of intellectual, structural, and relationship capital can be financially and competitively devastating and irreversible. This knowledge should influence companies to rethink what types of asset protection and value preservation resources should be developed, reframe how their intangible assets can most effectively be safeguarded and value preserved, and reconsider the origins, motives, and targets of the new insider.

Protecting Intangible Assets from the Insider Threat

Insider threats to information-based intangible assets, proprietary competitive advantages, and intellectual property represent persistent, global, nuanced, and frequently costly challenges to companies. In light of the economic fact that intangible assets are often in play and are integral components to business growth and transactions, all companies would be well advised to keep abreast of current insider threat research with an "eye" for fine-tuning and updating their best practice defenses.

Insider threat challenges, left unchecked or poorly addressed, go to the very heart of a company's value and sources of revenue. Such risks are unlikely to miraculously recede or fade away through attrition, terminations, or resignations absent the execution of best practices that thoroughly reflect the content of this chapter and can also adjust to current research—for example, knowing how the insider threats originate and evolve in companies, and knowing who the insiders are and their various motives. Research findings of that provide both a big picture and practical and relevant insights into insiders are being regularly produced by two institutions: Carnegie Mellon University's Insider Threat Research Center, and the U.S. DoD's Personnel Security Research Center (PERSEREC).

Both PERSEREC and Carnegie Mellon's definition of insider theft of IP share commonalities that I have converged as crimes in which current or former employees, contractors, or business partners intentionally exceeded or misused an authorized level of access to networks, systems, or data to steal confidential or proprietary information from an organization and variously use it in three primary ways: to get another job, help a new employer, or promote their own side business. A central theme underlying each motive is the insider's desire to achieve some form of personal financial gain.

Designing effective techniques to mitigate, counter, and ultimately defend against the insider threats should not be based solely on past practice, anecdotal (internal and external) snapshots, or generalized assumptions about ethnic allegiance. Rather defenses to the broad and complex phenomena of insider threats should be well grounded in relevant, current, and applied research.

Insiders: They Can Change from Date of Hire

By all accounts, the challenges of safeguarding valuable intangible assets in globally operating companies and the losses attributed to insiders is on the rise. The precise number of incidents companies experience, the dollar amount of those losses, and the end-use beneficiaries of the compromised assets are often blurred, incomplete, or have an agenda attached usually to elevate the dollar value of loss. This is because, among other things:

- Evidence remains subjective, anecdotal, or company specific that does not translate well to other sectors.
- Victim companies are frequently predisposed to assume the culprit is a foreign national or economic adversary.
- Instructive evidentiary elements of the incidents are classified.
- Facts about an incident are considered reputationally proprietary as well as embarrassing by the victim company.

Carnegie-Mellon University's Insider Threat Research (2005) Center identified the following attributes of an insider. This study was in regards to information technology sabotage, but I believe it can be extrapolated to other non-IT circumstances, particularly valuable and proprietary intangible assets.

1. *Access*: An insider can target a company from behind its perimeter defenses and not cause suspicion.
2. *Knowledge, trust, familiarity*: An insider has these things for both the IT system and the target, which permits insiders to perform discovery without arousing suspicion.
3. *Privileges*: An insider can readily obtain the necessary privileges necessary to conduct an attack.
4. *Skills*: An insider can mount an attack and can work within the target's domain expertise.

5. *Risk*: An insider tends to be very risk-averse in preparing for and conducting the attack.
6. *Method*: An insider is likely to work alone, but may recruit or co-op a trusted colleague for facilitation or enabling purposes.
7. *Tactics*: This may include either plant, hit, and run; attack and eventually run; attack until caught; or espionage.
8. *Motivation*: An insider may engage in an act for profit, getting paid to disrupt the target, provoke change in the company/target, blackmail, subvert the mission of the target, personal motive, or revenge.
9. *Predictable processes*: The motivation for an attack by an insider can evolve from a particular event, a sense of discontent, being "planted" to conduct the attack, or an adversary identifies a target and mission that meets their needs.

From these nine attributes of insiders who engage in IT sabotage two important questions arise:

1. Can these attributes relevant to insiders be consistently identified and assessed legally using existing pre-employment screening tools?
2. If the preceding attributes are not found to be present in an applicant at the time of hire, should companies, given the enormous stakes, invest in post-hire (periodic honesty, integrity, attitudinal) screening of employees to detect the presence of certain proclivities, propensities, or an overall receptivity to engage in adverse acts or policy violations affecting the security of their employer's information assets?

Threats to Intangible Assets from Insiders

Today's security practitioners are expressing equal concern about insiders as they are about outsiders breaking (hacking) in and stealing proprietary know-how according to various current studies and surveys. For example, in a survey by *Dark Reading* (a sister publication of *Information Week*) some of the key findings essentially buck a long-time trend among information security practitioners who have devoted a significant portion of their career (up to this point) addressing externally originated attacks to company data and proprietary information (Information Week Analytics, 2009). For example:

- 52% of the respondents reported they are more concerned now about probabilities of internal data leaks (both accidental and malicious) than they are about external threats.
- 44% reported just the opposite—that is, they're more concerned with external attacks than internal threats.
- 59% expressed belief that their organizations were either likely or bound to be infected in the coming 12 months with malware unintentionally introduced by internal employees and/or business partners.

- 52% said it is likely that an employee will accidentally expose sensitive company data/information to outsiders.
- 36% said it is likely that their organizations' sensitive data/information will be exposed due to loss or theft of a laptop or a portable storage device.
- 29% expect their IT employees to be caught abusing their access privileges for the purpose of looking at sensitive data/information that they are not authorized to see.

A 2008 Computer Security Institute survey (Richardson, 2008) reported that:

- 44% of all organizations experienced insider abuse of computer system.
- 42% reported laptop theft as now constituting an insider threat that is the third most common security event to organizations.

Another *Dark Reading* (2008) report found that most insider breaches are unintentional and are attributed to employees violating policies, circumventing security tools and practices.

In a study conducted by Insight Express and Cisco Systems (2008), it was found that almost 20% of users admitted to altering the security settings on company-issued devices so they could access unauthorized websites. In addition:

- 24% of these respondents further admitted to sharing sensitive company information with others.
- 44% admitted to allowing others to use their company-issued devices without supervision.

In the *Dark Reading* (2009) report it was revealed that employees can cause breaches (aside from losing laptops) in many different ways, some without realizing it. For example, insider breaches attributed to common user errors such as falling prey to phishing scams.

The Ponemon Institute (2013) in a recent study reported that negligence accounts for 88% of insider breaches, and malicious attacks account for only 12%.

Palo Alto Networks (2013) (a firewall vendor) conducted an analysis of insider threats to find that the source of several recent high-profile company-sensitive data/information breaches was due to the growing intentional employee disregard of company security policies that most larger firms are finding is unauthorized peer-to-peer application traffic.

"Houston, We've Got a Problem!": Unsecured Economies

Just how vulnerable are companies to having their proprietary intangible assets and intellectual properties stolen or compromised as a consequence to periods of economic downturn? According to a McAfee (2009) report the global economic crisis (recession) is quite literally creating a "perfect information security storm" as increased pressures on companies to reduce spending and cut staffing have led to more porous defenses and increased opportunities for cyber criminals.

It's certainly not unexpected to learn that the McAfee study found that the current economic stressors will exacerbate security issues for several reasons, one of which is that mass layoffs will influence a percentage of previously loyal employees to use their corporate data access to steal vital information.

The McAfee study found that:

- 68% of the respondents now cite insider threats as the top threat to vital information.
- 42% cite laid-off employees as the biggest threat caused by the economic downturn.
- 36% "worry about the security threat from financially strapped employees" (McAfee, 2009).

According to Tim Shimeall at Carnegie-Mellon, "With more sophisticated technologies at their fingertips and increased access to data, it has become easier for current employees and other insiders, such as contractors, consultants, suppliers, and vendors, to steal information. Data thefts by insiders tend to have greater financial impact given the higher level of data access, and, when combined with the effect of today's economic realities on IT security, this could mean even greater financial risk to corporations" (McAfee, 2009).

Ultimately, financial information becomes a recognized and sought-after currency for employees. It presents much greater incentives for employees to steal valuable information and data for personal financial gain, to try to improve their job opportunities by "peddling" it to unscrupulous or naïve competitors, or to literally start companies of their own by using the knowledge and insight they gained (stole) from their former employer.

In addition, the substantial cutbacks in company travel have, for all practical purposes, significantly curtailed or altogether ended onsite visits, inspections, personnel training, and audits for safeguarding a company's sensitive information assets. We can assume that in many instances, security practitioners are adapting to those realities by decentralizing and delegating their information asset protection and oversight role to onsite personnel.

Office of National Counterintelligence Executive

Since 1995, the Office of the National Counterintelligence Executive (ONCIX) has been mandated to gather data and submit an annual report to Congress on the state of foreign economic intelligence collection, industrial espionage, and export control violations.

Data for the report is collected from government agencies that comprise the U.S. counterintelligence community. What is particularly new in ONCIX's most recent report (Office of the National Counterintelligence Executive, 2011) are remarks regarding the increasing new modes of communication and social networking that provide uncharted opportunities for transferring information, and spying by enterprising foreign intelligence services. Also, companies encouraging outsourcing of their R&D and establishing foreign bases of operation, providing foreign entities with more opportunities to target U.S. information and technologies. A consequence is that it is increasingly difficult to accurately measure the extent of espionage and illegal acquisitions of U.S. trade secrets.

These and other studies, for many of us, prompt additional questions about economic and competitive-advantage adversaries, including insiders. There is a need to identify and assess factors that are related to employee reactions to the intensity and frequency of being targeted and solicited by external adversaries to engage in theft, misappropriation, or economic espionage of proprietary know-how and intellectual property. Certain factors can affect an employee's propensity to engage in information asset theft or economic espionage, by encouraging a receptivity to external buyers and solicitors of intangible assets, and/or prompt them to actively independently seek out prospective buyers.

If such propensities are contemplated and coincide with or become exacerbated by conventional motivators, such as disgruntlement, unmet expectations, personal predispositions, or personal finance stressors, the challenges presented by these threats become more acute and immediate.

One potential "patch" to these threats is that the complexities of personnel policies, procedures, practices, laws, and monitoring must be revisited. In the interim, companies should give favorable consideration to adopting a mode of sustaining control, use, ownership, and monitoring the value, materiality, and risks to their proprietary intellectual and structural capital—that is, their intangible assets.

References

Information Week Analytics, September, 2009. Analytics Brief: What Keeps Security Pros Awake At Night?

Carnegie Mellon University, 2005. Insider Threat Study: Computer System Sabotage in Critical Infrastructure Sectors. Software Engineering Institute. May, 2005.

Dark Reading, 2008. Report: Understanding The Insider Threat.

Dark Reading, 2009. Reports: Security Pros Shift Attention From External Hacks To Internal Threats. <www.darkreading.com/...security-pros-shift-attention-fr/215801195>.

Dyson, E., 1995. Intellectual Value, Wired Magazine, Issue 3.07, July, 1995.

Herbig, K., 2008, December. Allegiance in a Time of Globalization. PERSEREC Technical Report 08-10.

Insight Express and Cisco Systems, 2008. Data Leakage Worldwide: Common Risks and Mistakes Employees Make. Cisco Systems' commissioned study by InsightExpress.

Kramer, L. Heuer, R., Crawford, K., 2005. Technological, Social, and Economic trends that are increasing U.S. Vulnerability to Insider Espionage. PERSEREC Technical Report 05-10; also published as America's Increased Vulnerability to Insider Espionage, 2007. Int. J. Intell. Counterintelligence, 20, 50–64.

McAfee, 2009. Unsecured Economies: Protecting Vital Information: The first global study highlighting the vulnerability of the world's intellectual property and sensitive information. Santa Clara, CA.

Office of the National Counterintelligence Executive, 2011. Foreign Spies Stealing U.S. Economic Secrets in Cyberspace: Report to Congress on Foreign Economic Collection and Industrial Espionage. 2009–2011, Washington, D.C.

Palo Alto Networks, 2013. The Application Usage and Threat Report: An Analysis of Application Usage and Related Threats Within An Enterprise. 10th Edition.

Ponemon Institute Survey, 2013. The Risks of Insider Fraud. Cost of Data Breach Study in the United States. <www.ponemon.org/news-2/23>.

Richardson, R., 2008 Computer Security Institute, Computer Crime & Security Survey. Robert H. Smith School of Business at the University of Maryland.

Intangible Asset Strategist and Risk Specialist

Ascendance of Intangible Assets

If you're like me, you want to know what prompts or influences certain phenomena to occur. One of the first and perhaps most influential early studies on intangible assets was Brookings Institutes' "Understanding Intangible Sources of Value (1998–2000)". However, for all the forward-looking insights gleaned from this study and the product of its various working groups, it wasn't intended to provide readers with the underliers of why intangible assets evolved so rapidly at the outset of the 21st century.

As Baruch Lev (2005) from NYU's Stearn's School of Business stated so well, "If intangibles are so risky, their benefits so difficult to measure and secure, and their liquidity (tradability) so low, how did they become the most valuable assets most companies possess?" The answer, Lev suggests, lies in two international economic developments: the increasing intensity of business competition, and the commodization of physical assets.

The first international economic development that influenced the ascendance of intangible assets was the deregulation of particular economic sectors, such as transportation, financial services, and telecommunications. This served to intensify the **145** overall competitive global business transaction environment. As competitiveness intensified, a demand for continual innovation evolved—that is, the development and introduction of new products, services, and cost efficiencies. Thus, continual innovation quickly came to be a requisite to not merely competitiveness, but successful business operations and sustainability. As the global competitive pressures intensified further, companies already in the mix, or those that aspired to be, responded by engaging in more innovation, fueled, in large part, by greater awareness, appreciation, and investment in intangible assets.

The second international economic development that influenced the ascendance of intangible assets was the commodization of physical assets. This means that competitors globally had access to the physical assets that were now so necessary for becoming global in scope. For example, the physical assets of FedEx, DHL, and UPS became globally operational, almost simultaneously. Companies worldwide would now have access to instaneous supply and distribution chains for their goods and products. Therefore, a truly global and more timely marketplace could evolve, and did so quite rapidly.

However, as competitors globally gained equal access to physical assets, it meant that those assets, now engaged in intense competition, would not, standing alone, generate extraordinarily high profits and create sustained values. Rather, profits and elevated shareholder value would come to be created through the prudent use of intangible assets unique to, for example, each air cargo carrier. Each carrier then developed their own distinctive bundles, combinations, and synergies of intangible assets that better enabled them to withstand and respond more aggressively to the competition. Obviously today, all three air cargo carriers remain intact and compete against each other.

All Things Intangible: Starbucks

Intangible asset strategists not only see all things intangible, but they also see all things intangible in a different context. For instance, near my home is a Starbucks, and, as is the case for many Starbucks, it is located on a corner of a well-traveled intersection, so visibility is high. This Starbucks appears to be doing a bristling business, particularly its drive-thru operation. But, as is the case with many Starbucks' locations, it falls short on available parking for customers who prefer to purchase their beverage at the counter and use their facilities. Therefore, with regularity, customers seeking entrance to the drive-thru lane are stacked up in the queue that extends in to the adjoining street, frequently blocking both lanes and even the intersection of the main thoroughfare.

There are two adjacent commercial properties that Starbucks customers, somewhat as a default, regularly use for temporary parking in lieu of jockeying for a place in the drive-thru line. The rationale is that it simply takes less time to obtain your coffee this way. Interestingly, the proprietor of the closest adjacent commercial property—an independently owned and operated dry cleaners, which is largely dependent on customers in the immediate vicinity and which has ample parking, far exceeding what their employees and customers would ever require—elected to have a fence erected between their parking area and Starbucks, which precluded Starbucks customers from continuing to use that parking area to access their coffee.

Here is where the intangible assets apply, particularly relationship capital, reputation, image, and goodwill. Had the dry cleaner proprietor thought about these assets before erecting the fence, they could have created a "win–win" situation that would potentially boost their drying cleaning customer base and sales.

Let's set aside for the moment the probability the dry cleaners' liability insurance policy may have influenced the decision to erect the fence that precludes Starbucks' customers from using the back portion of the dry cleaners' parking lot to access their coffee. The proprietor of the dry cleaners, probably in collaboration with their insurance carrier and legal counsel, instead could have decided to "play nice."

That is to say, they could have posted a pleasant sign at the entrance to the parking area that would include both welcoming and warning language, such as "Starbucks' customers are welcome to use the back parking area at their own risk for a period of time sufficient to access Starbucks for the purpose of making their beverage purchase." They also could include signage specifically designed to increase traffic and customers to their dry cleaning establishment through some manner of minimal reward, such as a redeemable coupon upon showing of a Starbucks' receipt.

The proprietor of the dry cleaners would certainly build goodwill and enhance their community image and reputation all through a very inexpensive method of attracting new customers. At first though, this example may appear to some as "small potatoes." But, it prompts businesses and their management team decision makers to look at circumstances through an intangible asset lens.

Being engaged in the intangible asset arena for more than 20 years, I strongly believe that one need not look for examples only among large Fortune 500 companies; instead, examine and study the smaller and simpler examples, comparable to the examples cited here, and translate or convert them for application to other larger circumstances or their Fortune 500 distant cousins.

All Things Intangible: Yahoo!

Several years ago when Google's president Steve Balmer decided to bid on the purchase of Yahoo!, it was reported in various media that his last bid was for $43 billion and change (Computer World, 2011). Claiming no special insight as to the correctness of that figure, I can only assume it to be in the realm of possibilities.

Regardless what the real purchase price was, some colleagues in the intangible asset community estimated that, at minimum, $38 billion of the $43 billion was indeed comprised of various intangible assets.

That estimate seems to be aligned with global social media giants such as Twitter and Facebook that we understand have made no conventional profit, but their value, recent IPOs aside, largely consist of conglomerations of intangible assets.

Absent a larger organizational resilience, that leaves social media firms very receptive and vulnerable to an assortment of reputation-related risks, perhaps in some respects akin to a "bubble" that may or may not burst at some future point. Regardless, should I be asked, I would recommend security, asset protection, and value preservation resources are focused on reputation risks.

Intangible Asset Strategists and Risk Specialists Need to Work in Unison

For companies that wish to remain operationally effective and profitable with respect to the development, utilization, and exploitation of their intangible assets, asset strategy and asset risk management must function in unison. The most significant benefits an intangible asset strategist and risk specialist can contribute to companies are the following:

1. They provide ongoing best-practice guidance to companies, to ensure intangible assets are effectively positioned to extract value and deliver competitive advantages. They also develop strategic plans for asset utilization and exploitation.
2. They add predictability to business transaction outcomes, projected returns, and exit strategies when intangibles are in play, by addressing their stability, defensibility, and value sustainability.
3. They conduct assessments and due diligence to identify and unravel the contributions that are projected to be brought to a transaction are positioned to do so.
4. They reduce the probability that project or transaction momentum will be stifled by recognizing and mitigating circumstances that can entangle the assets in costly and time-consuming legal challenges, undermine asset value and performance, and adversely affect asset reputation, regulatory compliance, product and service quality, or security breaches.
5. Incorporate specialized knowledge management to facilitate an intangible asset-focused company culture aligned with a company's mission and business objectives.
6. Design comprehensive organizational resilience plans that encompass mission-essential intangible assets to provide quicker economic recovery following a significant business disruption or disaster.

7. Identify and monitor the interconnectedness between the production, acquisition, and utilization of intangible assets through their contributions to company value, revenue, and creating and sustaining competitive advantages.

Intangible Asset Oversight and Management

The 2006 Delaware court decision for *Stone v. Ritter*, as well as comparable decisions emerging from In re Caremark International Inc. (1996) and In re Walt Disney Co. Derivative Litigation (2005), drew much warranted attention to the necessity to consistently provide practical context to company boards regarding fiduciary responsibilities, including the oversight, management, and stewardship of company assets, with specific implications for intangible assets (see Demetriou and Olman (2007), Hill and McDonnell (2007), and Miller, 2008 for more information).

In other words, management teams and boards are obligated to be kept apprised of what is going on inside their company. For instance:

- In the form of good faith duties and duties of loyalty.
- To ensure their company has sufficient asset monitoring and reporting systems in place to routinely and properly keep them apprised through timely, sufficient, and accurate information.
- To allow them within their respective scope to reach informed judgments concerning a company's compliance with law and business performance.

Therefore, instead of remaining content with the past practice of having little substantive information about intangible assets, or assuming all things intangible fall exclusively to legal, accounting, or auditing and thus are not business strategy or risk decisions, management teams have fiduciary obligations to critically and objectively assess their company's assets.

It's useful for management teams to frame their intangible assets and IP as strategic business assets, not merely the product of a specific research activity that will remain stagnant or hidden, and otherwise not positioned for revenue-generating objectives.

The Convention of Pursuing Patent-Only Strategies

Having been engaged in countless meetings and engagements with a wide variety of innovators, researchers, and management teams, I am inclined to conclude that a business that engages in a patent-only strategy may be unfamiliar with the necessary preparatory aspects that skilled intangible asset strategists can contribute. Rather, they opt to first engage IP legal counsel.

These situations are frustrating for many intangible asset strategists, but are also elements firmly embedded in the minds, emotions, and marketing initiatives of entrepreneurs and experienced business persons alike. Another lies in the assumption that once an individual or company has their innovation, new product, or service, their next stop on the innovation success highway is to secure patent counsel and make application for a patent. See Chapter 7 for more detail regarding a patent-only strategy and the TRIPS agreement.

A challenge with a patent-only approach is that business management teams may overlook, undervalue, and project somewhat of a dismissive attitude toward the contributory intangible assets embedded in every patent application. Such dismissive attitudes are often rooted in the time-honored convention that an issued patent singularly conveys ownership, certain rights, and provides legal standing for asset defensibility under the law.

However, as has been noted, the legal and administrative costs associated with obtaining and maintaining a patent are not insignificant, not to mention the extraordinary costs necessary to pursue infringers and counterfeiters or defending a patent against allegations of infringement. These costs continue to escalate, making the patent-only tract increasingly out-of-reach for smaller companies in particular.

Intangible asset strategists and risk specialists can provide company decision makers – strategic planners with viable options for safeguarding their companies' intangible assets at the earliest stages of asset development and/or acquisition aside from conventional forms of intellectual property enforcements.

References

Computer World, October 18, 2011. IDG News Service. Perez, J.C.

Demetriou, A., Olman, J., 2007. Stone v. Ritter: The Delaware Supreme Court Affirms the Caremark Standard for Corporate Compliance Programs, Vol. 3. American Bar Association Health eSource, Number 6.

Hill, C., McDonnell, B., 2007. Stone v. Ritter and the expanding duty of loyalty. Fordham Law Rev. 76 (3), Article 17.

In re Caremark International Inc. Derivative Litigation, 698 A.2d 959 (Del. Ch. 1996).

In re Walt Disney Co. Derivative Litigation 907 A.2d 693 (Del. Ch. 2005).

Lev, B., 2005. Intangible Assets: Concepts and Measurements. Encyclopedia of Social Measurement, Volume 2. Elsevier.

Miller, R., 2008. Wrongful Omissions by Corporate Directors: Stone v. Ritter and adapting the process model of the delaware business judgment rule. Univ. Pennsylvania J. Busi. Employ. Law, 10 (4), 911–940.

Understanding Intangible sources of value, 1998–2000. The Brookings Project, Co-Directors: Margaret Blair and Steve Wallan and the Intangible Research Project, Co-Directors: Baruch Lev and Phillip Bardes, NYU, Stearn School of Business.

Intangible Assets in 2014 and Beyond: Where Businesses Must Be

Recognizing How and Where Intangible Assets "Fit"

Recognizing how and strategizing about where and when intangible assets "fit" in every company's 2014 and beyond strategic business planning is a resolution that will guarantee favorable outcomes and returns.

An essential starting point is management team consensus, intellectually and operationally, in the economic fact that more than 80% of most companies' value, sources of revenue, and building blocks for near-term and sustainable profitability and growth lie in or evolve directly from intangible assets.

As noted numerous times, far too often and quite unfortunately this economic fact, and intangible assets in general, are dismissed by management teams who either lack understanding, harbor reservations for some reason, or simply don't possess the inclination to unravel the embedded and sometimes camouflaged benefits and multipliers that well-nurtured intangible assets will almost surely deliver to a company. One rationale for maintaining such indifference to intangible assets is that a percentage of management teams are quick to dismiss them as being too esoteric or, worse, irrelevant to *their* company, and the types of business transactions they typically engage in. Such disregard is now and will be even more indefensible as intangible assets achieve greater permanency in all aspects of business operation and performance measurement.

One thing is for sure, for 2014 and beyond, any remnants of unfamiliarity or reluctance among company decision makers, strategic planners, and management team members to fully and consistently engage their intangible assets—that is, understand how to utilize them best for their contributory value—will ensure their company remains behind rather than ahead of the business curve.

Designing A Sturdy and Malleable Plan to Engage Intangible Assets

The following represent key features I believe are essential and recommend that management teams should consider. These features will help with conceiving, designing, and executing a sturdy, but malleable plan for aggressively and consistently engaging and making a company's intangible assets integral factors to every project, initiative, or transaction.

- Bring operational clarity to intangible assets by having a repertoire of relevant examples applicable to a variety of industry sectors.
- Bring contributory value clarity to intangible assets.
- Draw attention to the importance of practicing consistent stewardship, oversight, and management of intangible assets, framed as highly fiduciary responsibilities, not merely irrelevant tasks.
- Explain why it's necessary to not just identify intangible assets, but unravel their origin, evolution, development, ownership, control, defensibility, sustainability, and contributory value.
- Seek and incorporate best practices to sustain control, use, and ownership, and monitor value, materiality, and risks to the assets throughout their respective value, life, and functionality cycles, and the contributory relevance of those tasks.
- Build an effective, yet readily maneuverable risk early-warning system with both prevention and criticality mitigation features that reflect the speed with which adverse acts can evolve to erode asset value and competitive advantages.
- Describe how asset risks materialize as inadvertent or intentional reputation risks or are instigated by globally economic adversaries.
- Distinguish intangible asset valuation, contributory value, revenue conversion, and performance measurement in understandable economic contexts.
- Describe how to determine intangible assets' contributory fit to particular initiatives, projects, and transactions relative to the assets' functionality and value cycles, risks, and retaining or transferring use or ownership rights.

- Demonstrate relationships between the production or acquisition and use of intangible assets relative to how they produce multiplier-effects, elevate company value, and deliver competitive advantages, sources of revenue, and specific contributory value.
- Describe ways to position or bundle intangible assets, particularly those producing higher levels of contributory value, as a strategy to achieve a broader base for leveraging and strengthening competitive advantages, and elevating value.
- Avoid reliance on subjective worst-case-scenario anecdotes or tactics to convey asset risks as a strategy to attract attention.

The execution of any of these features, however, should include a company-wide intangible asset-awareness campaign that emphasizes a collective responsibility for three main principles:

- Asset identification, stewardship, oversight, and management
- Sustain control, use, and ownership, and monitor value, materiality, risk
- Assess assets' performance and contributory value

Each of these principles represents an increasingly essential element to achieving success to be measured by profitability, growth, brand, reputation, and sustainability.

Most company management teams already know that designing and executing a company-wide initiative to bring operational clarity and relevance to intangible assets will not be without challenges. The initial challenges manifest as realities—that is, intangible assets lack a conventional sense of physicality, and they are seldom accounted for on company financial statements.

The following sections outline some key factors that I recommend management teams should fully consider when designing the necessary business case for making their intangible assets an integral part of their business routine and strategic planning and positioning.

Example Why Intangible Asset Training Is Important

While teaching a graduate MBA course for a mid-western university several years ago, I purposefully sequenced my syllabus to reflect my determination to introduce students to intangible assets and strategies related to their management, stewardship, oversight, and risk mitigation. I feel strongly that intangible assets should be an integral teaching and learning component in every business management course, especially at the graduate level.

Once the class started and it was time to introduce intangible assets, I assured the students I was doing so not merely as an afterthought, rather as constituting an integral component to the course. It quickly became apparent that, for even the most experienced and already employed students, intangible assets had yet to become part of their business lexicon or repertoire of relevant skill sets other than in the context of independent assets for which it was difficult, at the initial stages, to recognize or differentiate their connection to a company's value, competitive-advantage production, profitability, growth, and sustainability. A percentage of students possessed a fundamental familiarity for particularly recognizable intangible assets, such as brand, reputation, and patents. But once I presented a laundry list of intangible assets, there was still a tendency of the students to characterize them in standalone contexts, not reliant on or connected to other company assets, actions, or events.

Upon completion of this course, student responses to the final examination essay questions related to intangible asset issues revealed numerous remaining challenges relative to achieving a sufficient grasp of intangible assets in several key areas:

- Intangible assets could be subject to a collective framework of management, stewardship, and oversight.
- To recognize intangible assets' contributory value to a company, particular product or service, or new product development.
- To relate and distinguish particular intangible assets as contributing to specific sources of revenue and competitive advantages.
- The assets could be vulnerable to various types of risk, which, if materialized, could erode company value and reputation.

An important initial hurdle to fully understanding the integral relevance of intangible assets lies in their intangible nature. That is, intangible assets lack a conventional sense of physicality, unlike tangible assets that one can see and touch, such as inventory, vehicles, buildings, and machinery. I sense the students' reactions and ability to grasp the management, stewardship, and oversight of intangible assets was a reflection of the larger business community and its management teams As this course progressed, most students appeared to concedethe role, function, and contributory value of intangible assets was not merely vaguely relevant, but actually important information to know. However, one particular student with a strong and optimistic career in financial services consistently challenged and resisted the position I was espousing regarding the relevance and contributory value of intangible assets across sectors.

This student was working in his institutions' large commercial loan and acquisition unit. He would describe numerous and significant loan and acquisition transactions in which, as he stated, there was absolutely no mention, recognition, or accounting of intangible assets in either valuation, collateral (securitization), or due diligence contexts.

At the conclusion of the last class, this student approached me and said, "I understand what you're saying Mr. Moberly, about intangible assets, but I just don't see intangible assets ever becoming an issue in my bank, as you suggest they should and eventually will, at least while the current bank officers remain in place. In my bank, it's solely about identifying and assessing the value of physical assets as collateral."

Of course, an important question to ask is, is this attitude held by a single large financial services institution representative of attitudes held by business management teams in other sectors regarding intangible assets? My answer to that question is yes, at the moment.

But, as in most instances when there is eminent change looming on the horizon, be it political, financial, social, or legal, it will inevitably prompt some level of resistance, particularly from people and institutions that are thoroughly embedded and comfortable with past practice. In other words, intangible assets remain somewhat of a hard sell.

There Are Intangible Asset "Rembrandt's" in Most Every Company's Attic That Can Become Profit Centers

Here's an interesting perspective offered by Ashok Jain (2004), a principal in the intellectual property valuation services unit of Deloitte. Jain suggests that interactions he has had with large U.S. companies lead him to draw the conclusion that while most profess a fairly high-minded level of IP prowess, relatively few can answer substantive questions about the management of their IP and intangible assets. For example:

- Does your company maintain an inventory of its patents?
- Which patents (IP in general) are core to business operations and the strategic plan?
- Is your company exploiting its IP and other intangible assets to generate the greatest possible value?

There are numerous companies, institutions, and individual management team members that have achieved impressive national and international reputations for being the originator of a new idea, which may eventually become lucrative intellectual property. However, a percentage of these individuals or companies may be reluctant to assume the hands-on and very personal risk associated with executing a new idea. Instead, it's reported that numerous idea generators may delegate the responsibility for stewarding and overseeing the actual development and execution of a new idea to either legal counsel or a CTO.

Jain explains one possible reason for this reluctance is that the technical and legal units of a company are frequently portrayed as cost centers, not profit-producing centers. Such characterizations give credence to the notion that idea generators recognize risk in achieving a return-on-investment for ideas related to safeguarding, preserving, monitoring, utilizing, and exploiting intangible assets.

Jain also suggests that probably a large (but unknown) percentage of companies knowingly give away or inadvertently relinquish valuable intangible assets and IP, and do not effectively use their intangible assets or IP to achieve competitive advantages, generate new sources of revenue, or otherwise favorably leverage the assets in any manner. This trend begs the question: Do these presumably unfavorable perspectives constitute a crisis relative to current practices in the management, stewardship, and oversight of any company's intangible assets? Companies and their leadership now have both a fiduciary and financial incentive and responsibility to acquire an operational familiarity with intangible assets. This includes the capability to identify, unravel, develop, safeguard, and fully apply their intangibles (Rivette and Kline, 1999).

Building Intangible Asset Sand Castles

I believe company management teams need to rethink how they're utilizing their intangible assets. This starts by not subordinating these increasingly valuable and strategic assets. Think of this as being akin to sandboxes, in which a little water can be periodically added to enable the building of temporary sand castles, the value and relevance of which will quickly crumble and dissolve into indistinguishable forms as the moisture evaporates or the tide changes.

This sand castle scenario carries particular relevance today, as so many businesses are on the leading edge of the knowledge-based global economy—that is, they have countless intangible asset building blocks that could deliver value, sources of revenue, growth, and sustainability. The bottom line is, management teams need to recognize their assets if they don't already, and engage them so they can be effectively applied and exploited.

This All Can Occur Quite Simply

Interestingly, this all can occur rather simply. That is, by ensuring the right parties, with the right expertise (i.e., intangible asset strategists and risk specialists), are received for what they do and say. For instance, new product development and design meetings should include intangible asset strategists and risk specialists. After all, the end game, of course, is to ensure that a company's investments in or acquisition of intangible assets, including intellectual properties and supporting R&D, blend effectively with a company's strategic business and market planning.

There is a growing number of management teams who not only "get it," but they are "getting it right," and that's a good thing! Admittedly, this may be preceded by occasional missteps, miscues, and even missed opportunities, most of which are not irreversible.

Unfortunately, regardless of the fact-based immanence of intangible assets playing increasingly key roles in most every business activity, I still see instances in which intangible assets are being pushed away from management and development to being legal, technical, and or compliance functions. This, of course, underlies the reason why such large percentages of IP and intangible assets go one way, while the R&D, CTO, legal counsel, marketing, and new product design groups go another way.

I often remark to business leaders that there remains a significant number of "Rembrandt's" accessible, available, and useable, but they're not all stored in a company's attic; rather, they're right in front of them. They merely need to be identified, unraveled, assessed, and put to work!

References

Jain, A., 2004. 'Talking Intellectual Property Seriously', Chief Executive, November 1, 2004, chiefexecutive.net/taking-intellectual-property-seriously#sthash.E7s3SM3Q.dpuf

Rivette, K.G., Kline, D., 1999. Rembrandt's in the Attic: Unlocking the Hidden Value of Patents, first ed. Harvard Business Review Press, Boston, Mass (November 15, 1999).

Further Reading

Sherman, A.J., 2011. Uncover Hidden Revenue in Your Company's Intellectual Property Harvesting Intangible Assets. AMACOM.

Index

159

Printed and bound by CPI Group (UK) Ltd, Croydon, CR0 4YY

08/05/2025

01864773-0001